TOP50 standards

Arranged by Dan Coates

Alfred Music
P.O. Box 10003
Van Nuys, CA 91410-0003
alfred.com

ISBN-10: 0-7390-6217-4
ISBN-13: 978-0-7390-6217-3

M000159856

TABLE OF CONTENTS

AS TIME GOES BY

(from "Casablanca")

Words and Music by Herman Hupfeld
Arranged by Dan Coates

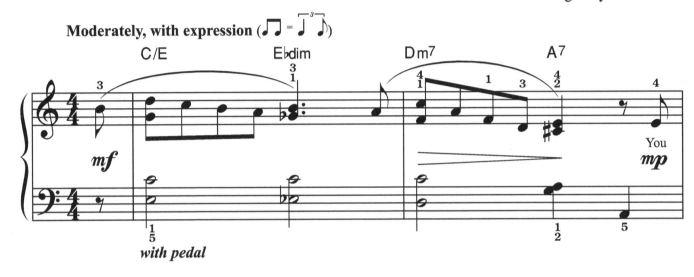

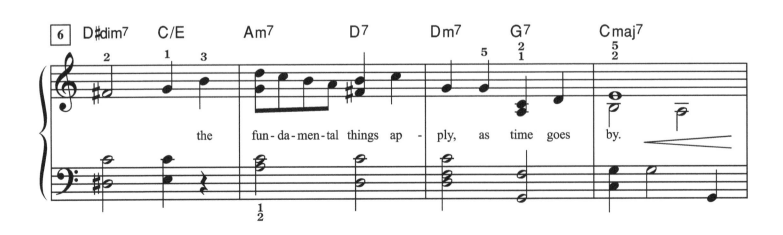

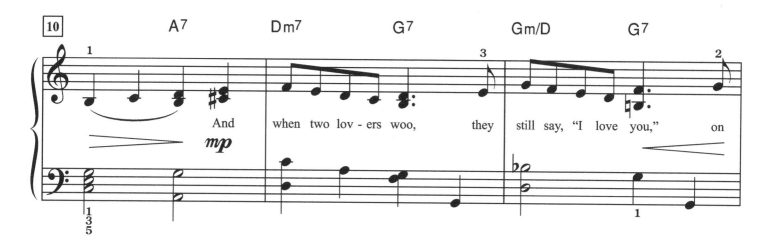

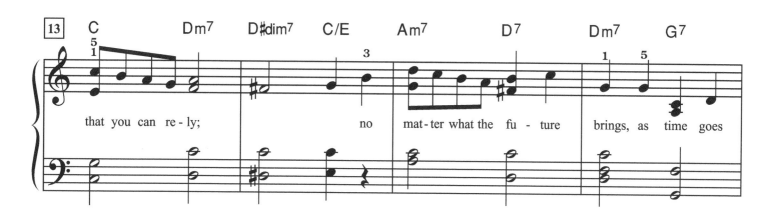

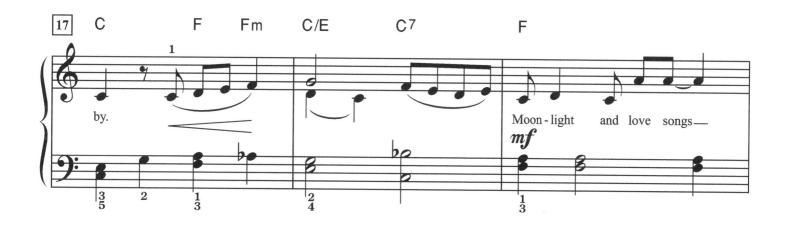

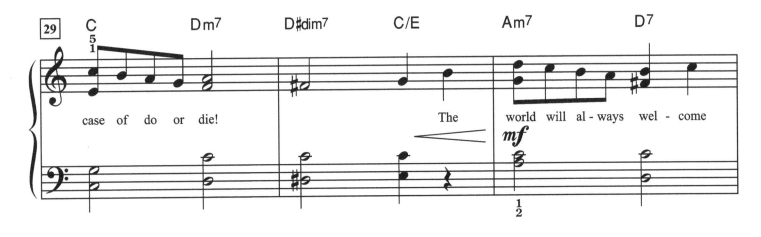

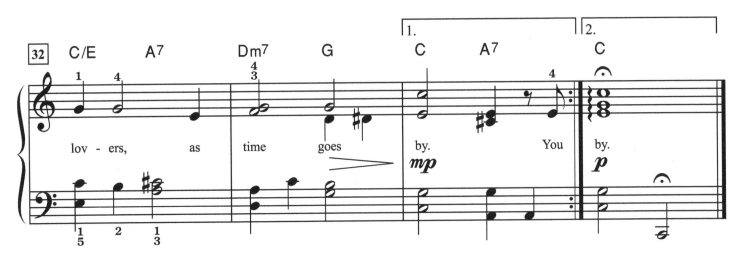

AT LAST

Music by Harry Warren
Lyrics by Mack Gordon
Arranged by Dan Coates

8

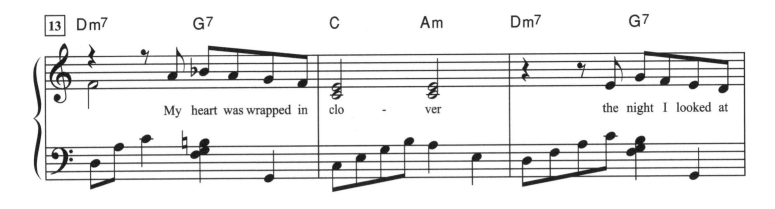

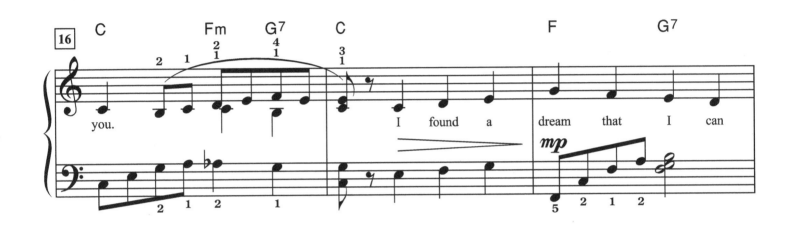

BEGIN THE BEGUINE

(from "Jubilee")

Words and Music by Cole Porter
Arranged by Dan Coates

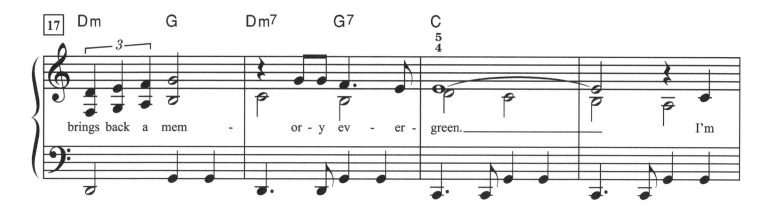

brings back a mem - or - y ev - er - green._____ I'm

with you once more_____ un - der the stars_____ and

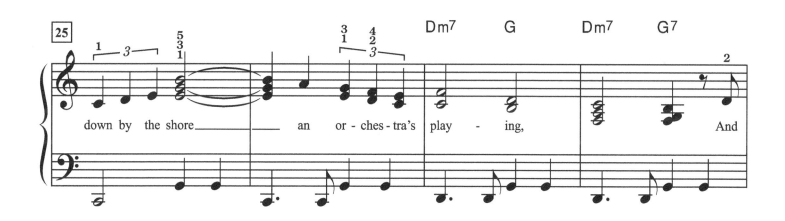

down by the shore_____ an or - ches - tra's play - ing, And

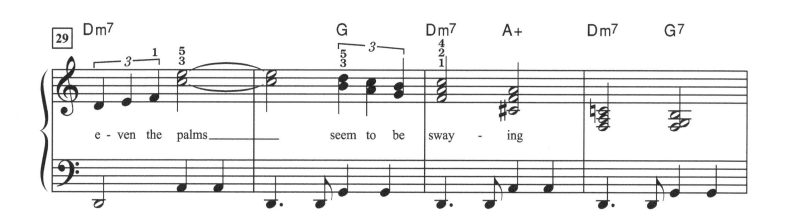

e - ven the palms_____ seem to be sway - ing

12

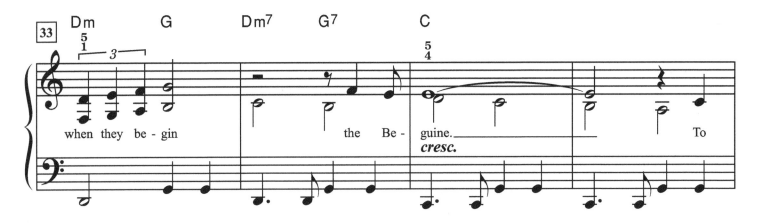

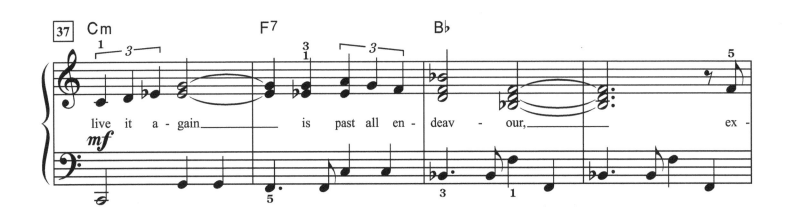

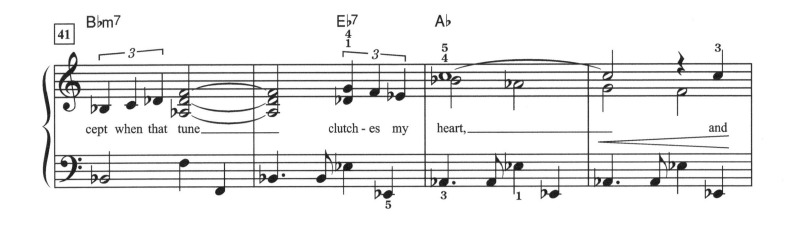

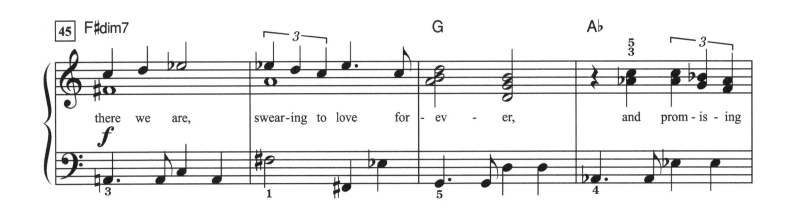

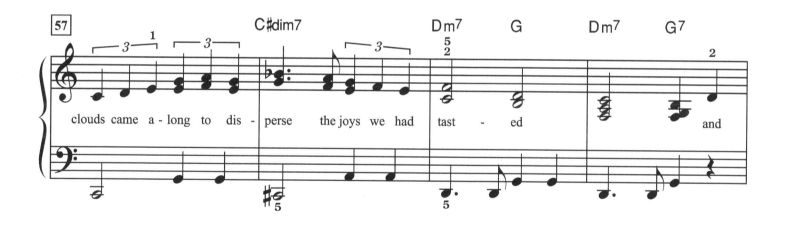

14

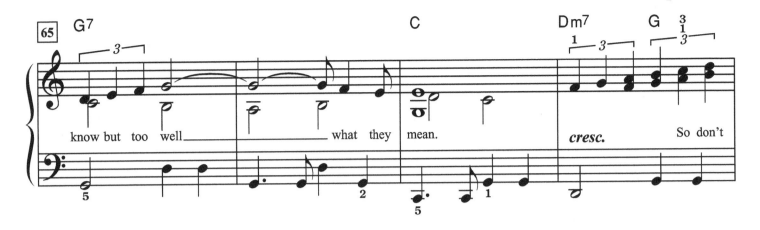

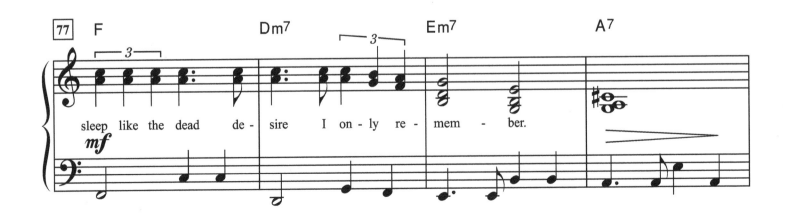

When they be-gin_____ the Be-guine. Oh yes,

let them be-gin the Be-guine, make them play_____ 'til the

stars that were there be-fore re-turn a-bove you,_____ 'til you

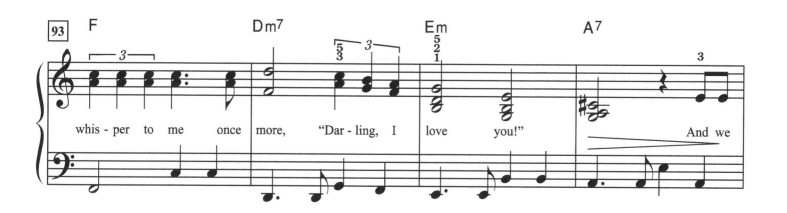

whis-per to me once more, "Dar-ling, I love you!" And we

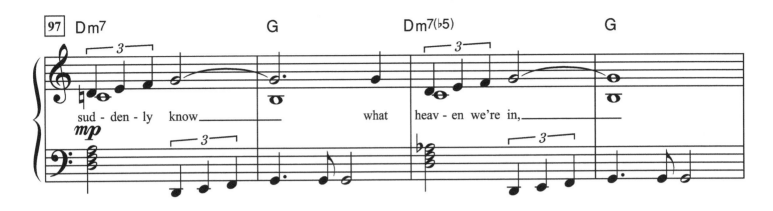

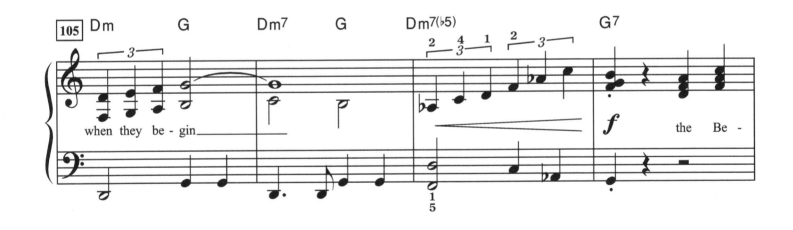

THE BEST IS YET TO COME

Music by Cy Coleman
Lyric by Carolyn Leigh
Arranged by Dan Coates

The best is yet to come— and, babe, won't it be fine,

you think you've seen the sun— but you ain't seen it shine.

Wait 'til the warm-up's un-der way,— wait 'til our lips have met,

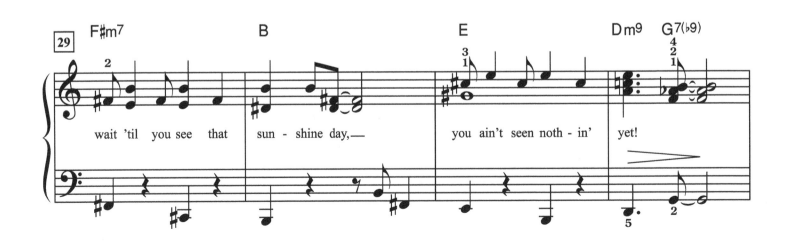

wait 'til you see that sun-shine day,— you ain't seen noth-in' yet!

The best is yet to come — and, babe, won't that be fine,

the best is yet to come, — come — the day — you're mine. Come — the day — you're

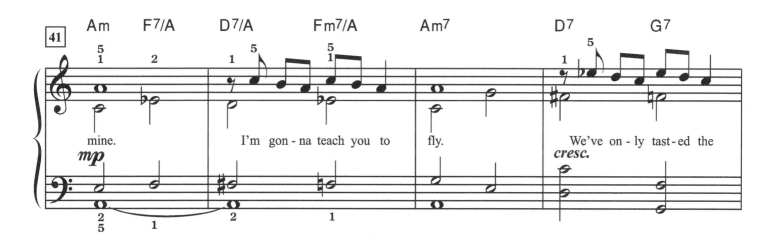

mine. I'm gon-na teach you to fly. We've on-ly tast-ed the

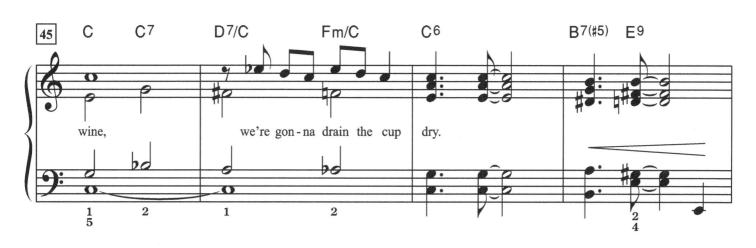

wine, we're gon-na drain the cup dry.

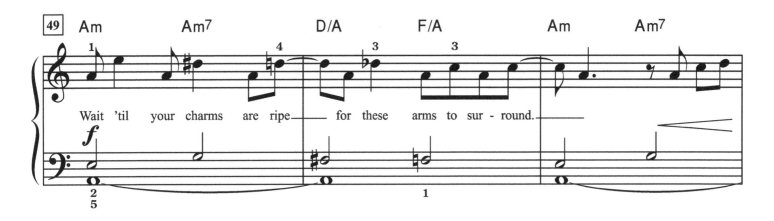

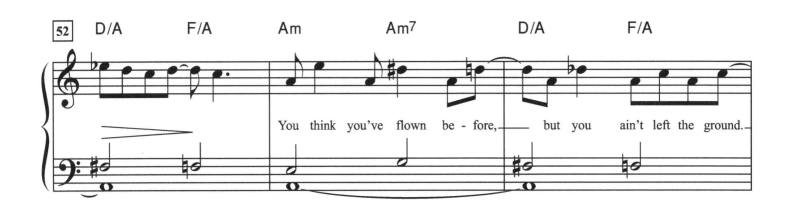

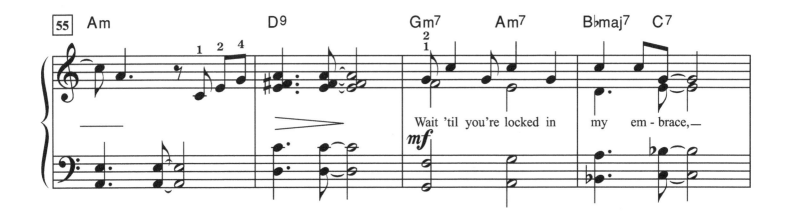

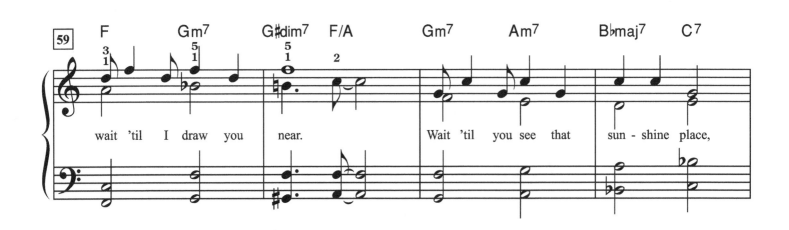

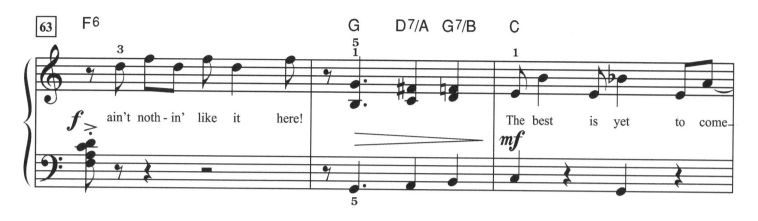

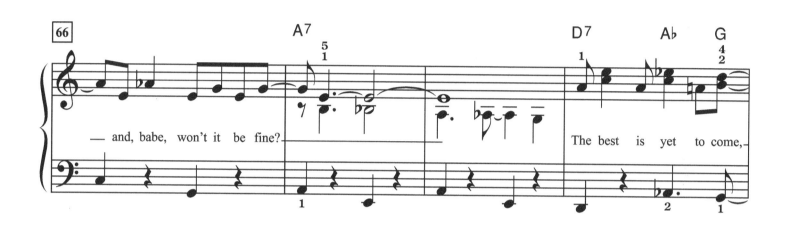

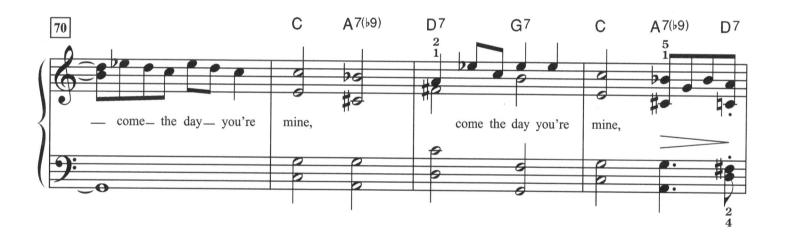

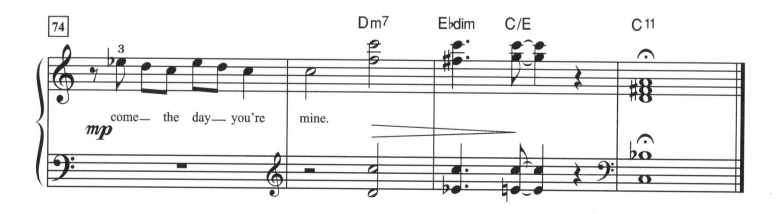

BEWITCHED, BOTHERED, AND BEWILDERED

(from "Pal Joey")

Words by Lorenz Hart
Music by Richard Rodgers
Arranged by Dan Coates

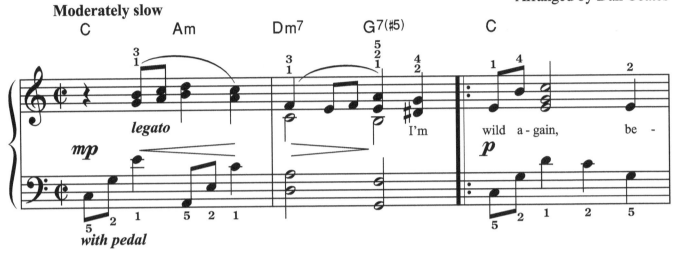

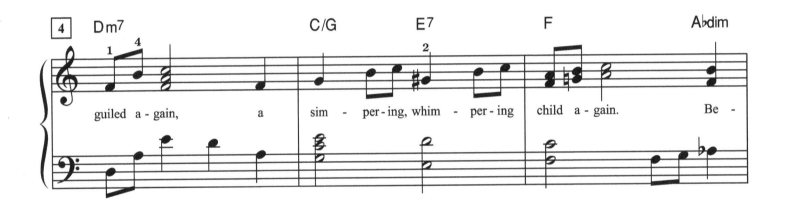

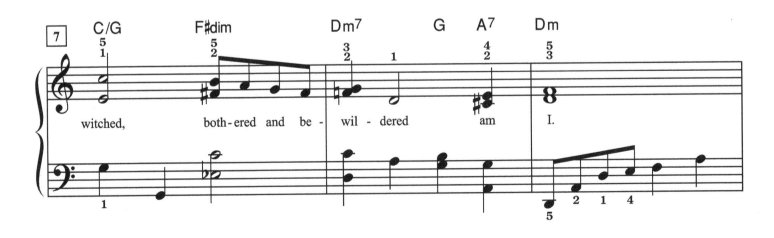

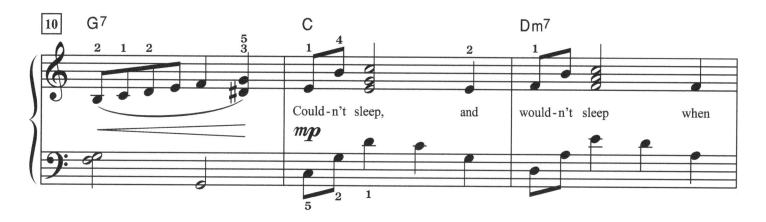

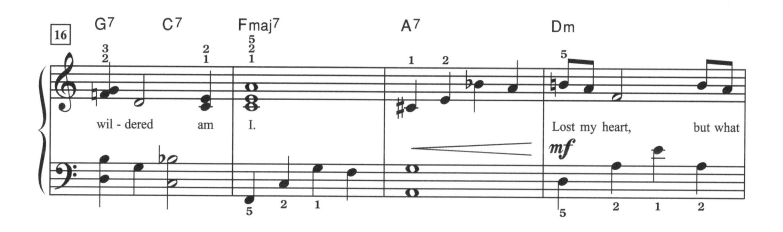

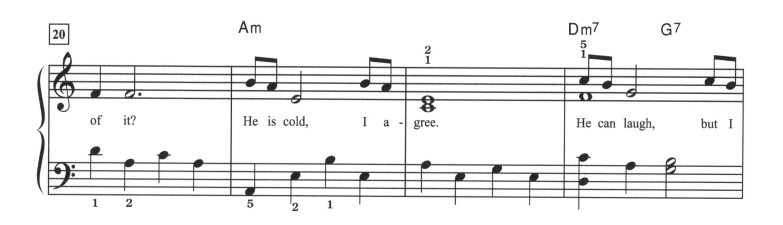

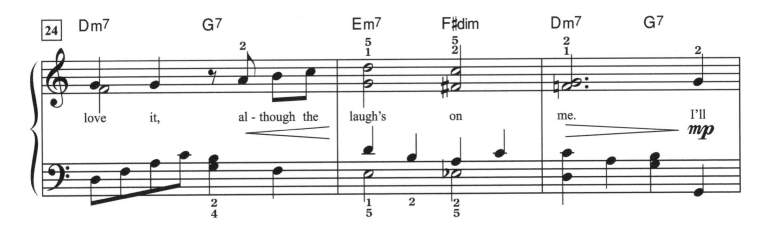

love it, al - though the laugh's on me. I'll

sing to him, each spring to him, and long for the day when I'll

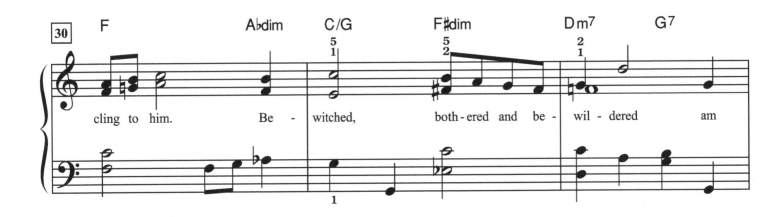

cling to him. Be - witched, both - ered and be - wil - dered am

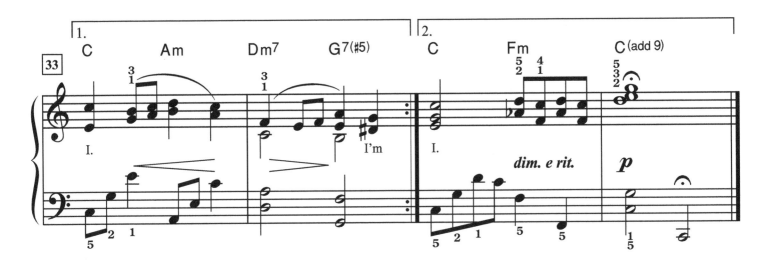

I. I'm I.

BUT NOT FOR ME

(from "Girl Crazy")

Music and Lyrics by
George Gershwin and Ira Gershwin
Arranged by Dan Coates

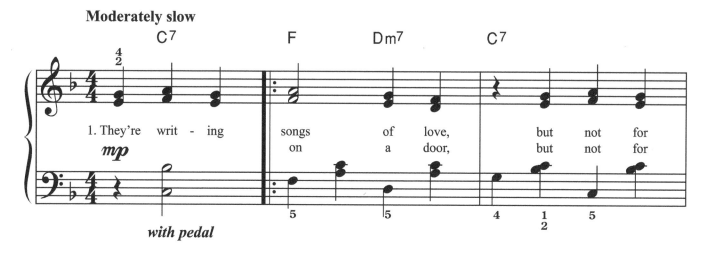

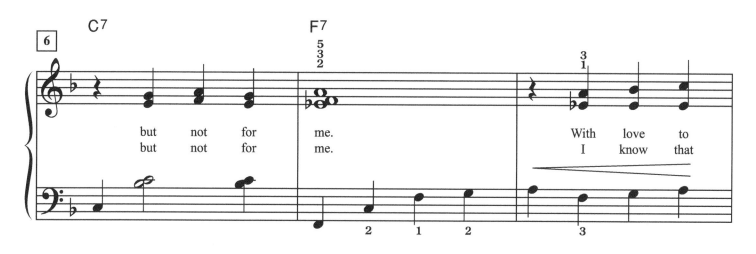

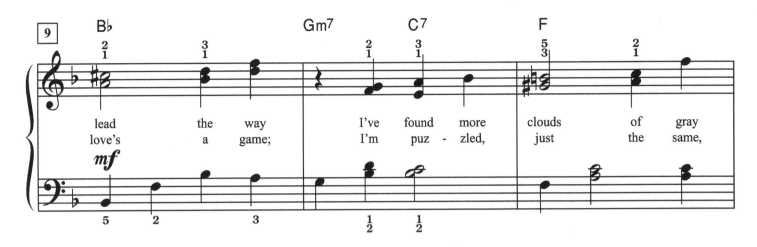

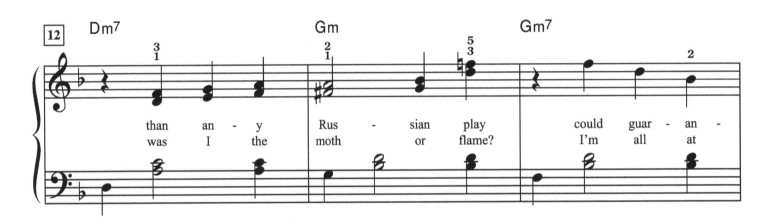

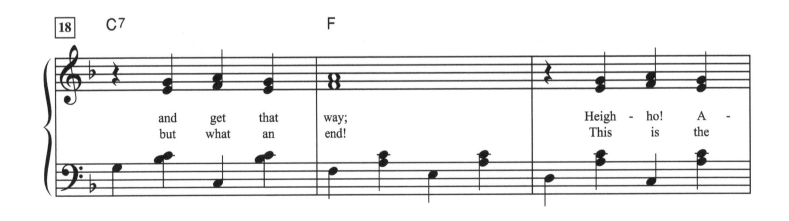

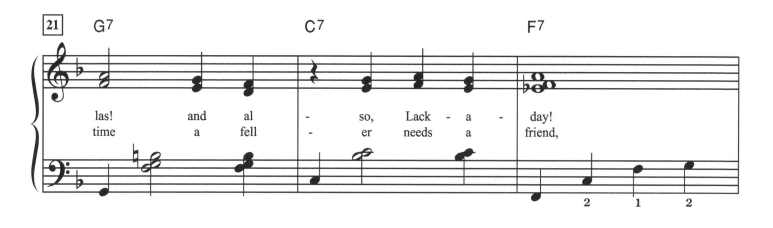

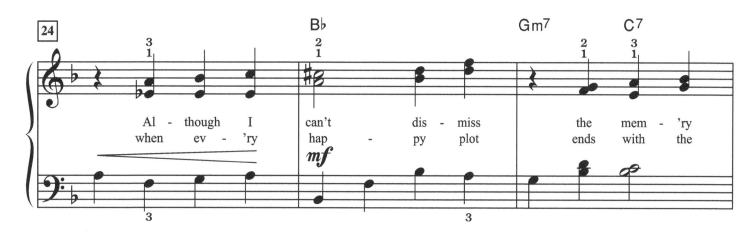

BLUES IN THE NIGHT

Words by Johnny Mercer
Music by Harold Arlen
Arranged by Dan Coates

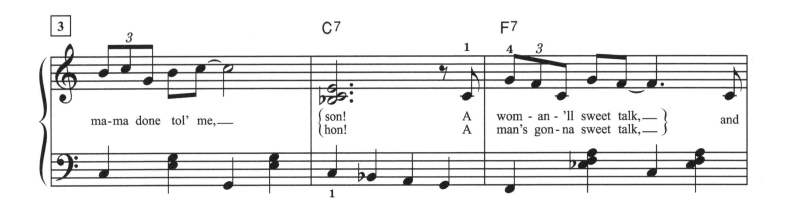

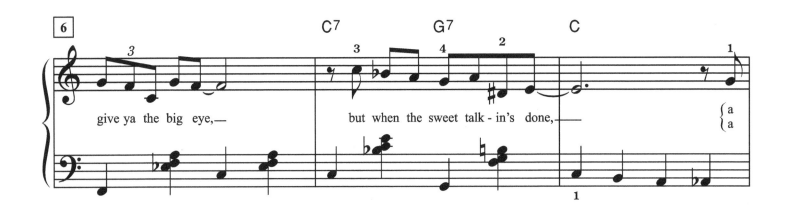

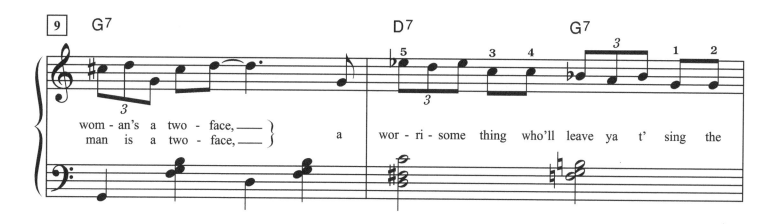

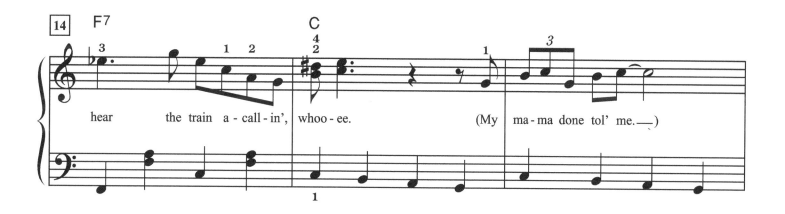

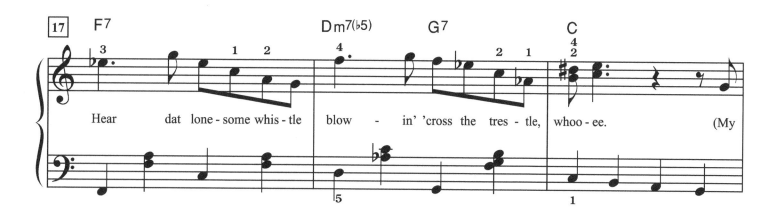

20

ma - ma done tol' me.___)　　A

G7

whoo - ee - duh - whoo - ee,___　　　　ol'

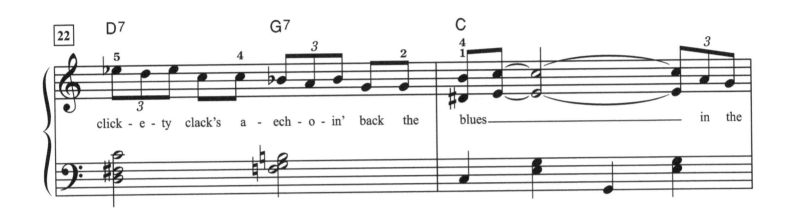

22　**D7**　　　**G7**　　　**C**

click - e - ty clack's a - ech - o - in' back the　blues___　　　　　in the

24

night.　　From Nat - chez to Mo - bile,___　from Mem - phis to St. Joe,___　wher -

mf

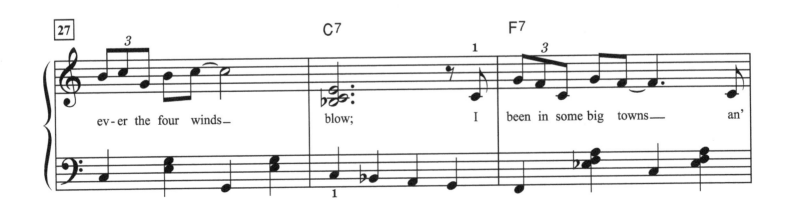

27　　　　　　**C7**　　　**F7**

ev - er the four winds___　blow;　　I been in some big towns___ an'

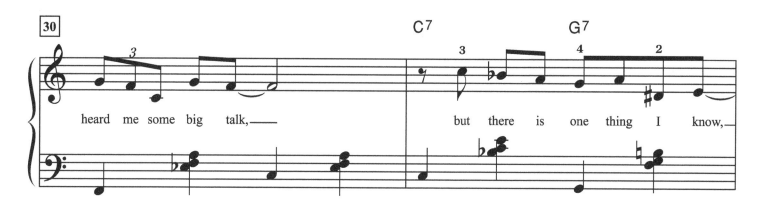

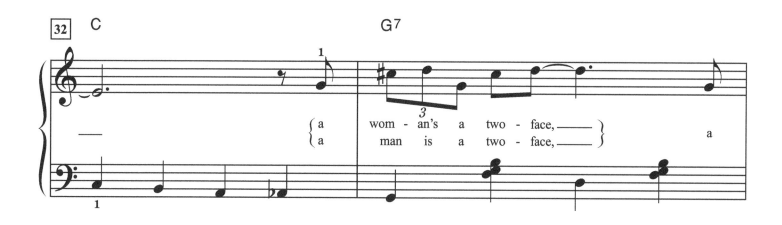

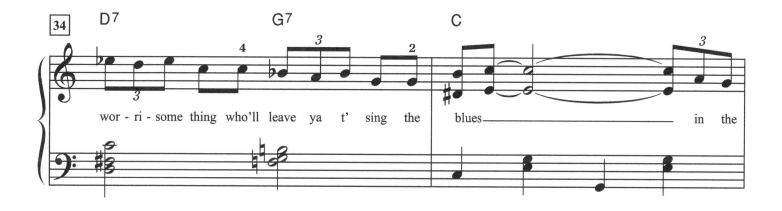

BRIDGE OVER TROUBLED WATER

Words and Music by Paul Simon
Arranged by Dan Coates

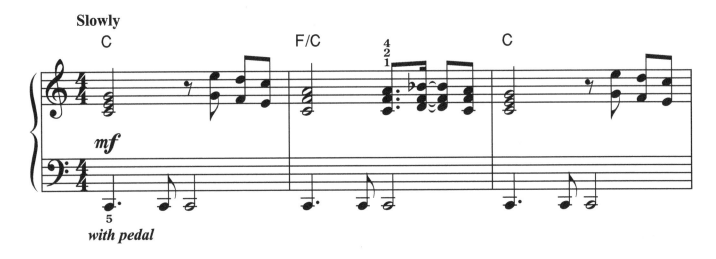

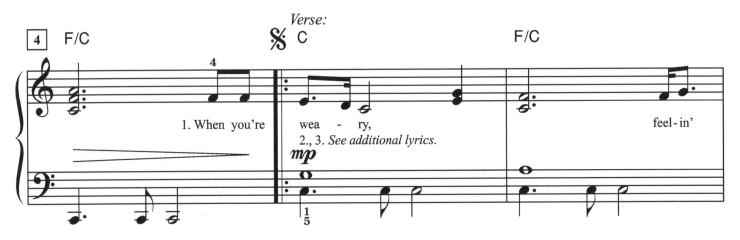

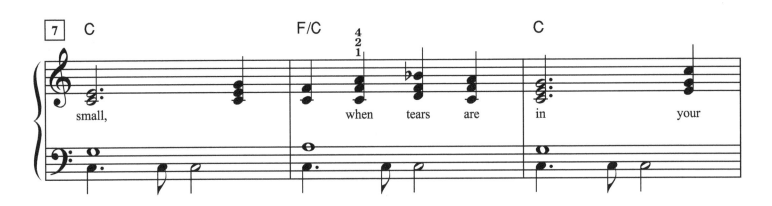

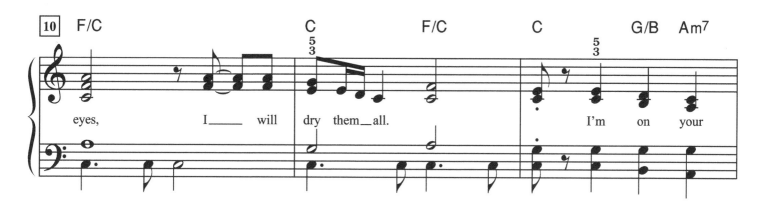

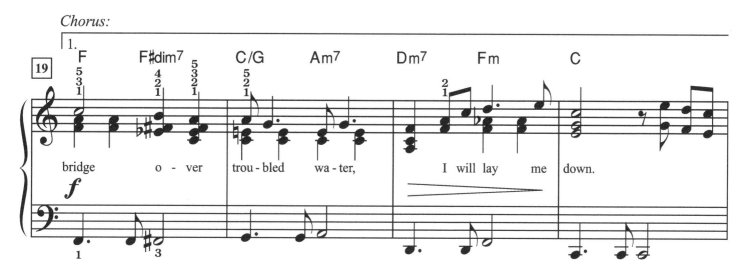

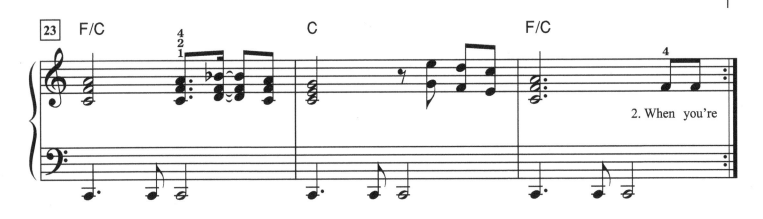

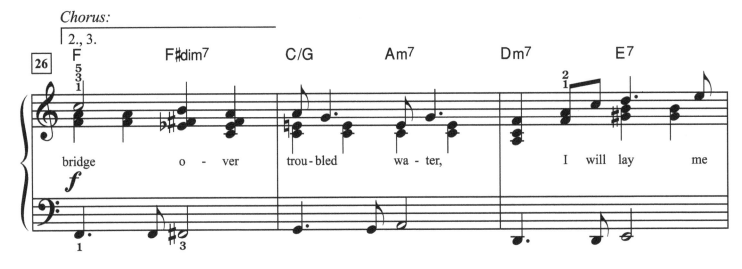

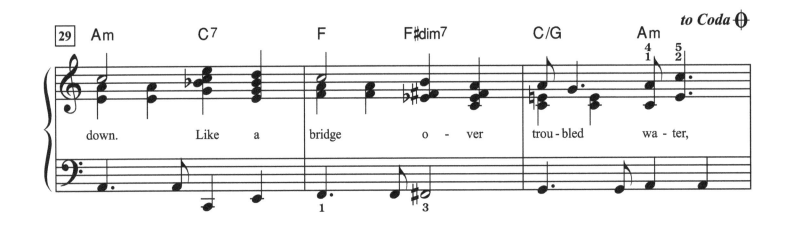

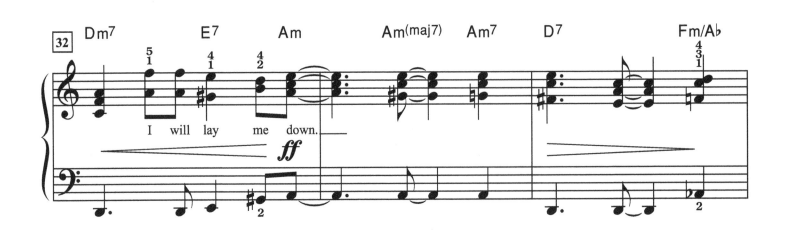

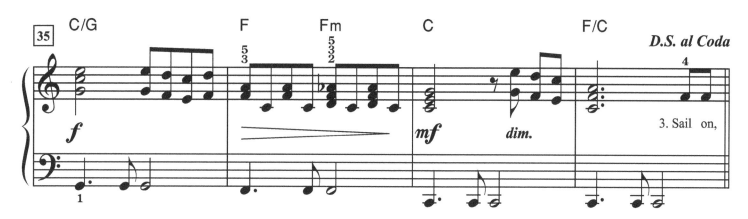

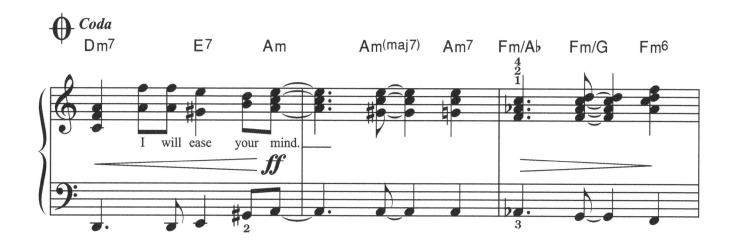

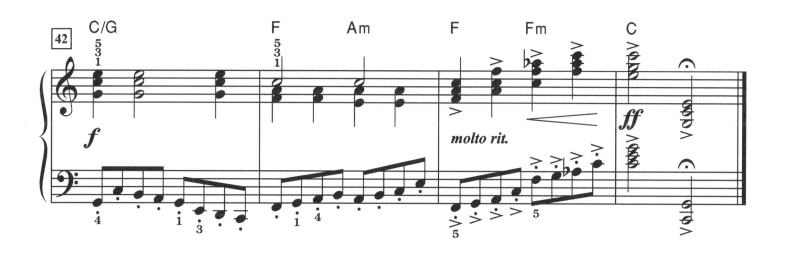

Verse 2:
When you're down and out,
When you're on the street,
When evening falls so hard, I will comfort you.
I'll take your part when darkness comes
And pain is all around.
Like a bridge over troubled water, I will lay me down.
Like a bridge over troubled water, I will lay me down.

Verse 3:
Sail on, silver girl, sail on by.
Your time has come to shine,
All your dreams are on their way.
See how they shine, if you need a friend.
I'm sailing right behind.
Like a bridge over troubled water, I will ease your mind.
Like a bridge over troubled water, I will ease your mind.

BYE BYE BLACKBIRD

Words by Mort Dixon
Music by Ray Henderson
Arranged by Dan Coates

Slowly, with feeling

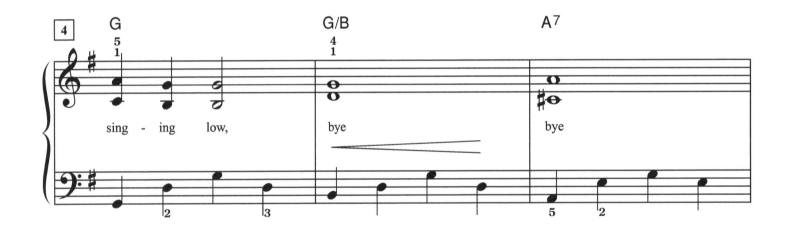

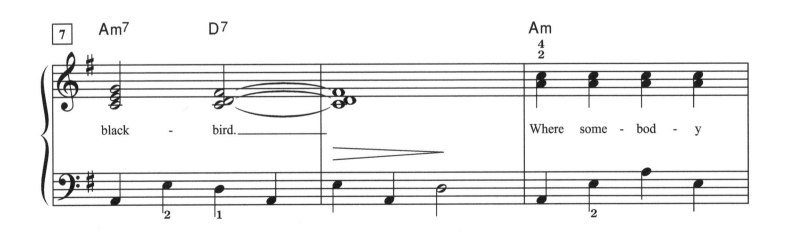

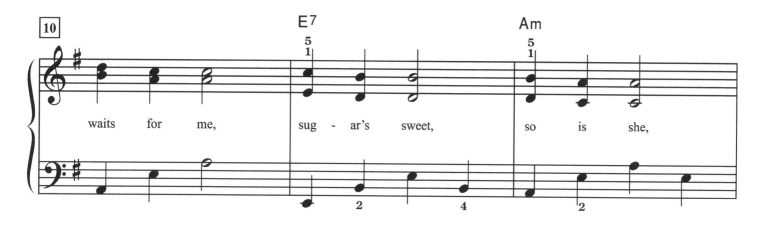

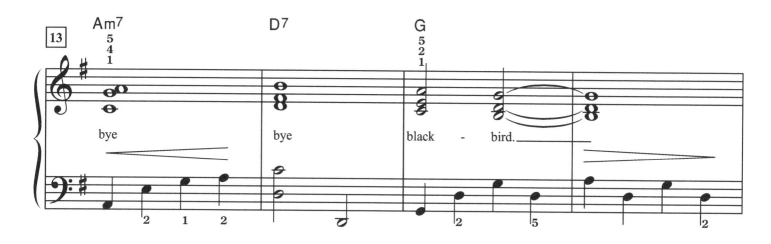

DANNY BOY

Traditional
Arranged by Dan Coates

CHATTANOOGA CHOO-CHOO

Music by Harry Warren
Lyrics by Mack Gordon
Arranged by Dan Coates

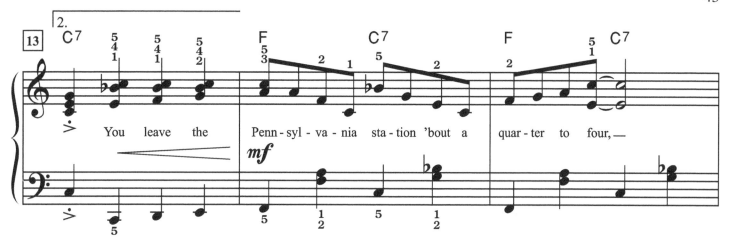

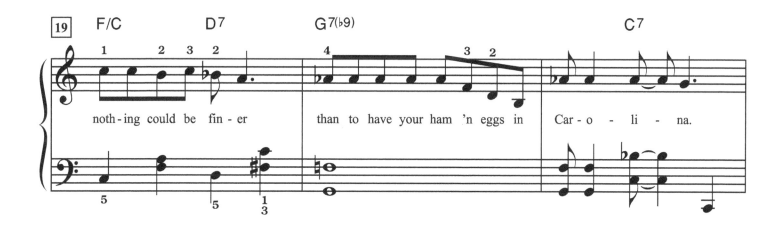

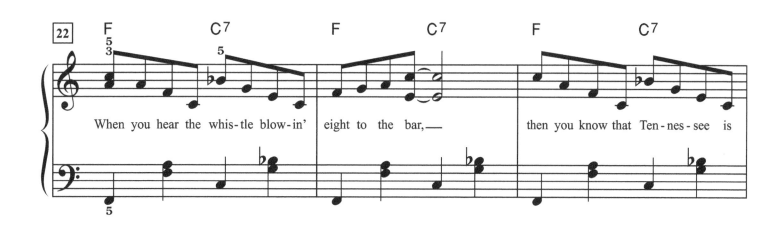

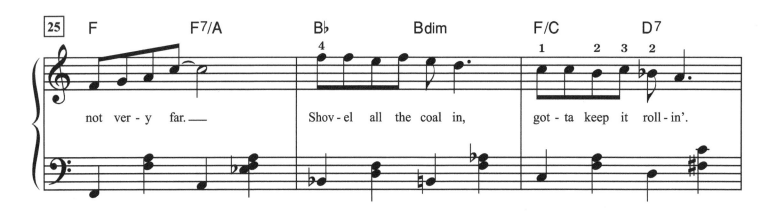

not ver - y far. —— Shov - el all the coal in, got - ta keep it roll - in'.

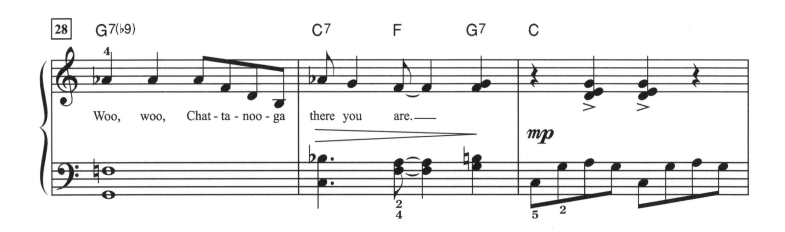

Woo, woo, Chat - ta - noo - ga there you are. ——

There's gon - na be —— a cer - tain par - ty at the

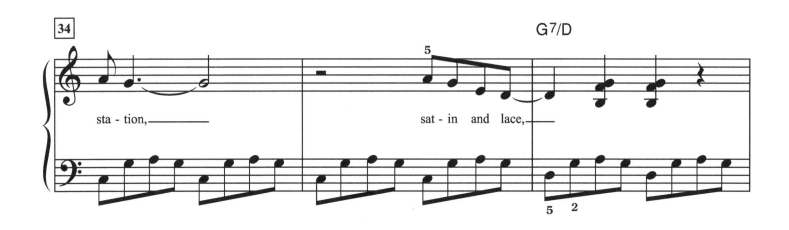

sta - tion, —— sat - in and lace, ——

THE DAYS OF WINE AND ROSES

Lyric by Johnny Mercer
Music by Henry Mancini
Arranged by Dan Coates

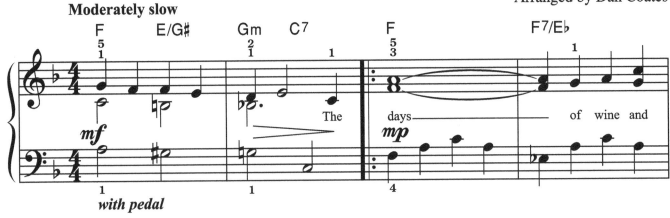

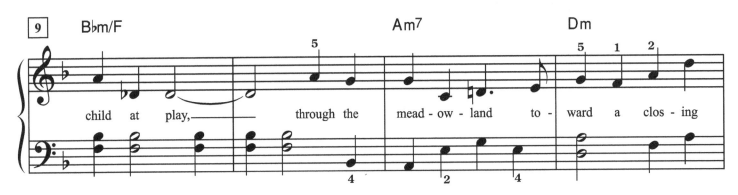

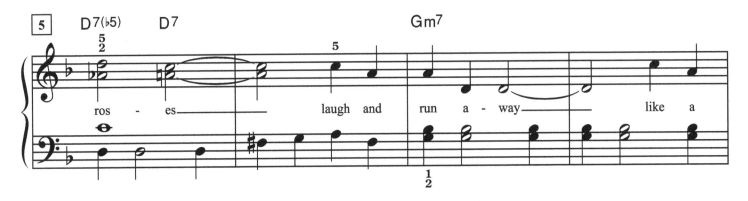

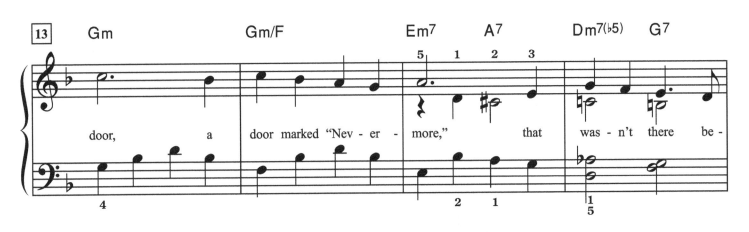

DON'T GET AROUND MUCH ANYMORE

Music by Duke Ellington
Lyrics by Bob Russell
Arranged by Dan Coates

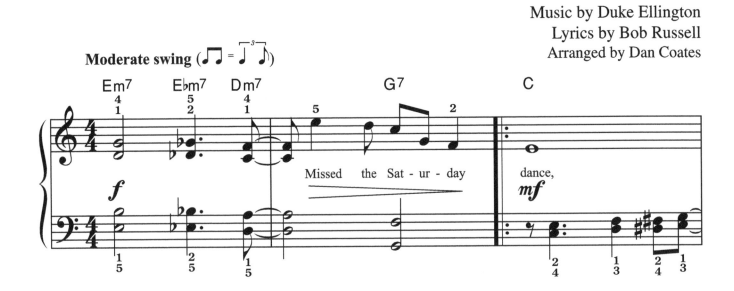

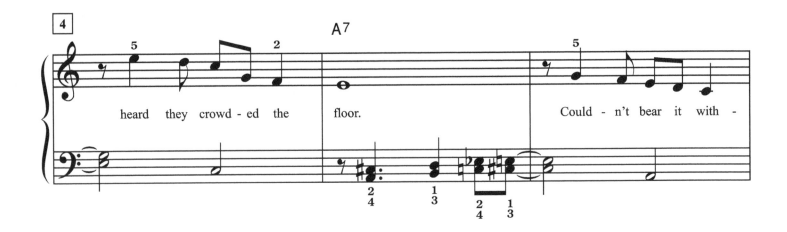

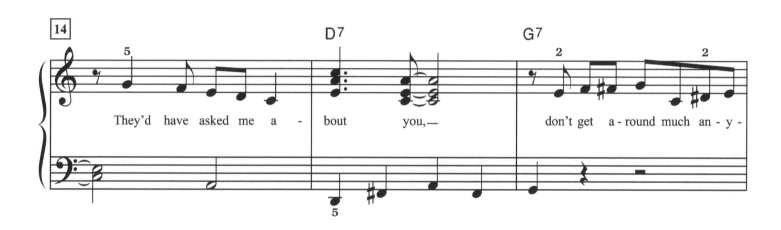

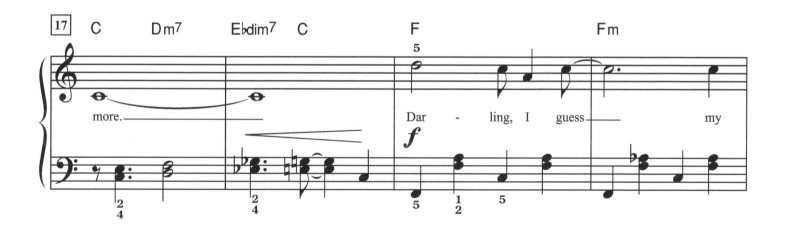

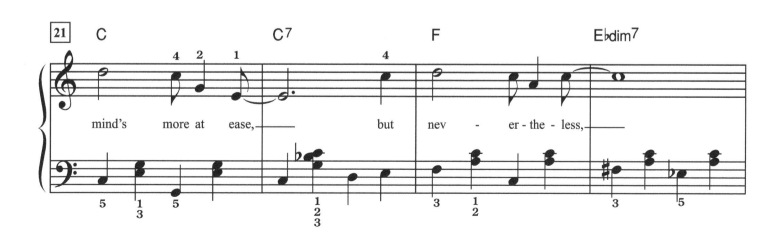

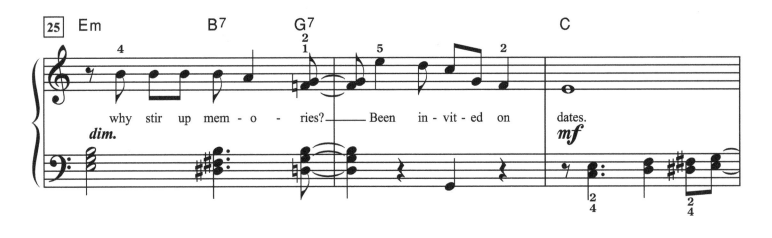

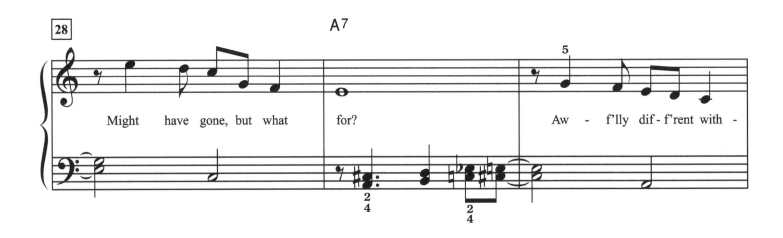

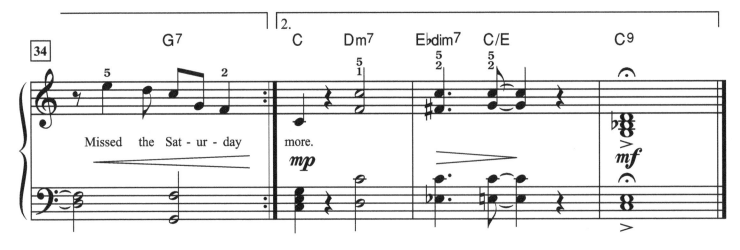

EMBRACEABLE YOU

(from "Girl Crazy")

Music and Lyrics by
George Gershwin and Ira Gershwin
Arranged by Dan Coates

Moderately slow, with expression

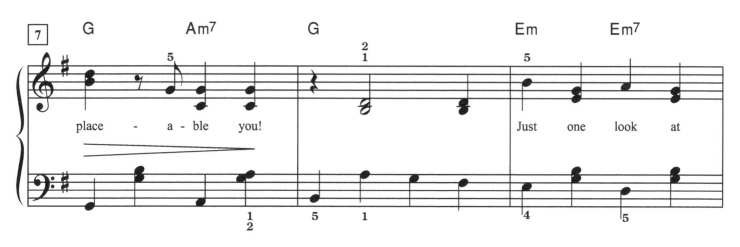

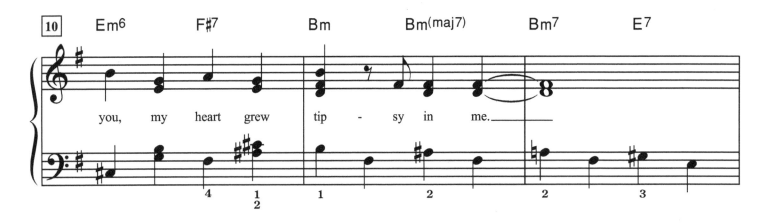

10 Em⁶ F#7 Bm Bm(maj7) Bm7 E7

you, my heart grew tip - sy in me._____

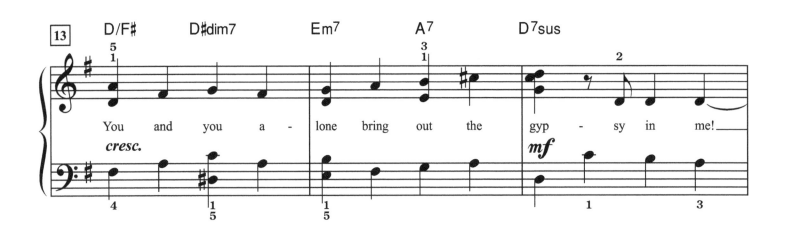

13 D/F# D#dim7 Em7 A7 D7sus

You and you a - lone bring out the gyp - sy in me!_____

cresc. *mf*

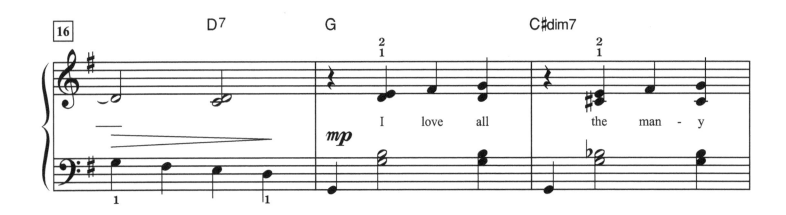

16 D7 G C#dim7

I love all the man - y

mp

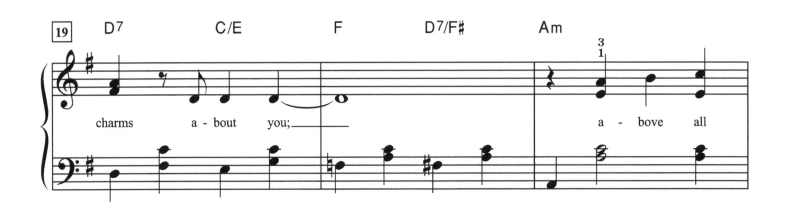

19 D7 C/E F D7/F# Am

charms a - bout you;_____ a - bove all

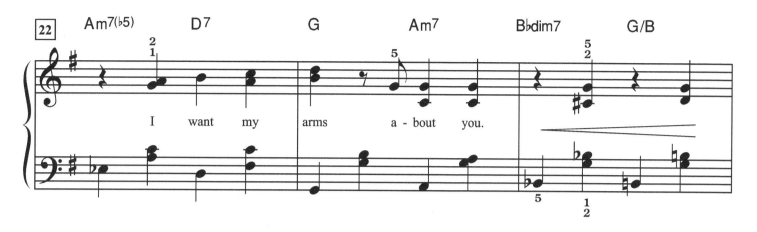

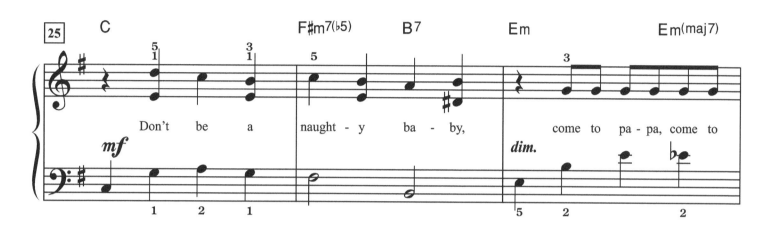

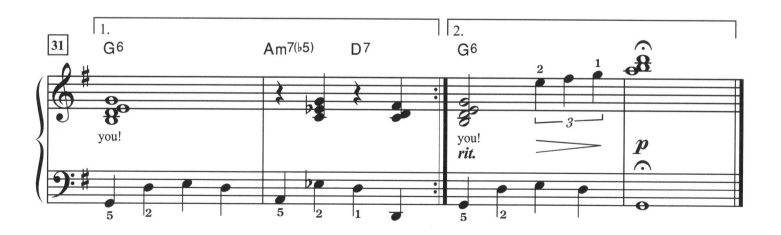

EVERGREEN

(Love Theme from "A Star is Born")

Words by Paul Williams
Music by Barbra Streisand
Arranged by Dan Coates

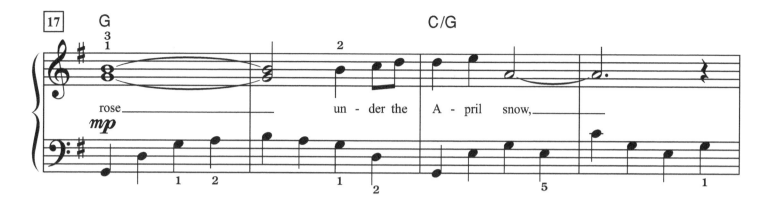

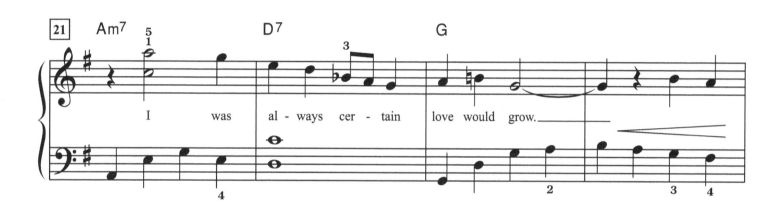

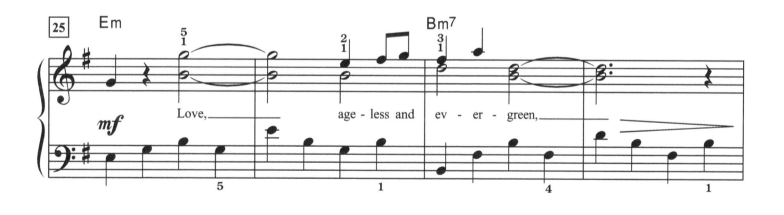

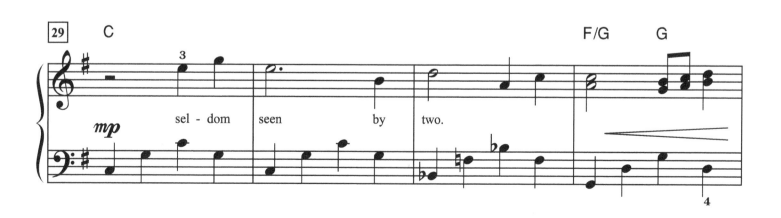

THE ENTERTAINER

By Scott Joplin
Arranged by Dan Coates

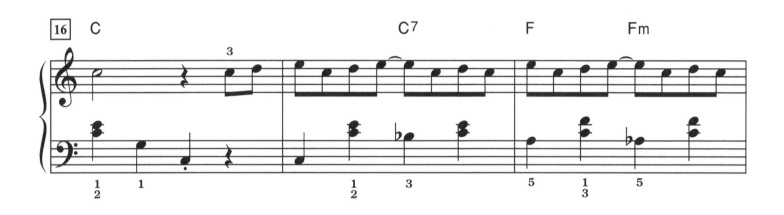

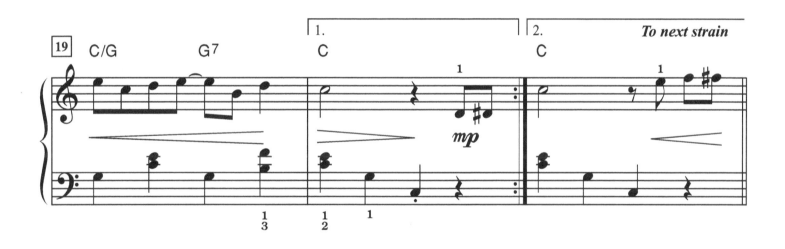

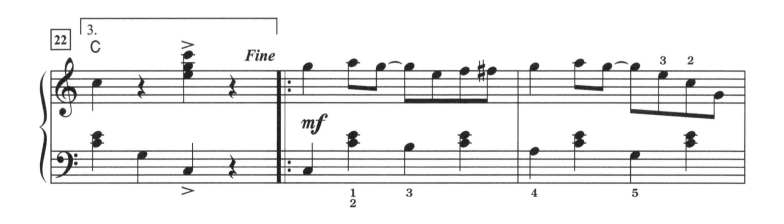

FLY ME TO THE MOON
(IN OTHER WORDS)

Words and Music by Bart Howard
Arranged by Dan Coates

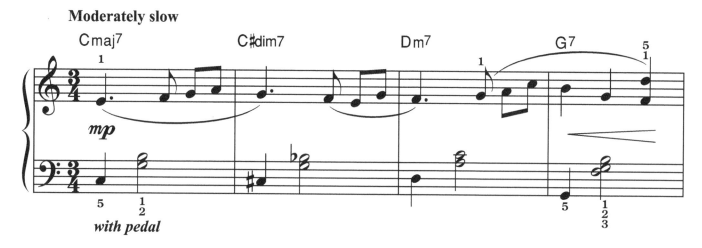

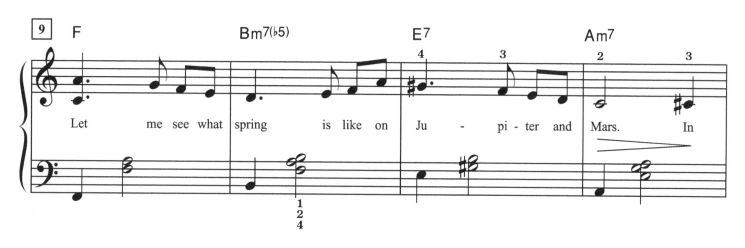

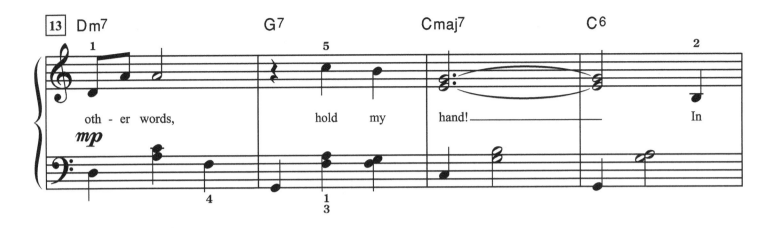

oth - er words, hold my hand! _____ In

oth - er words, _____ dar - ling, kiss me!

Fill my heart with song and let me sing for - ev - er more;

you are all I long for, all I wor - ship and a - dore. In

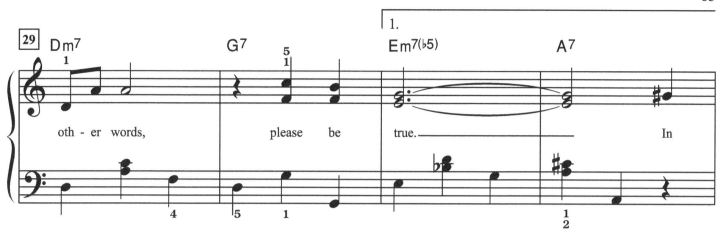

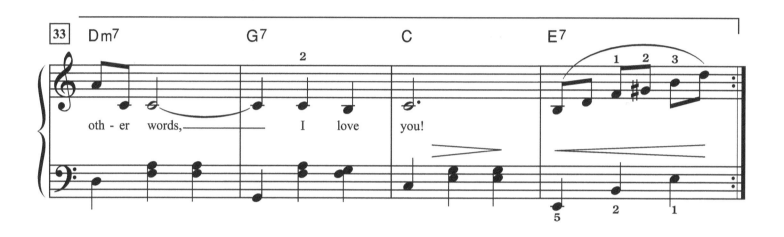

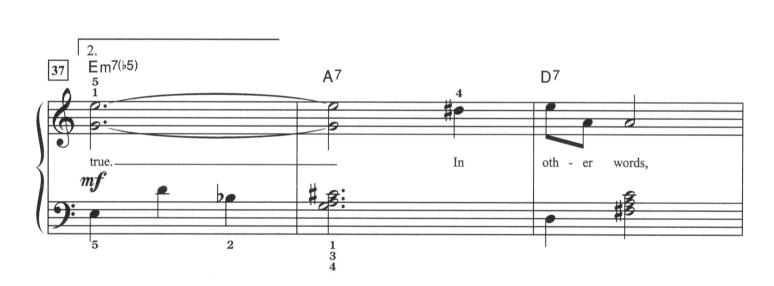

I COULD WRITE A BOOK

(from "Pal Joey")

Words by Lorenz Hart
Music by Richard Rodgers
Arranged by Dan Coates

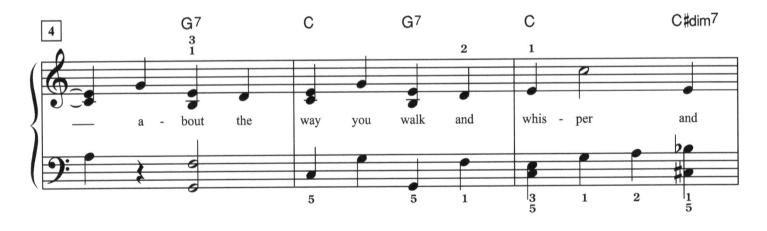

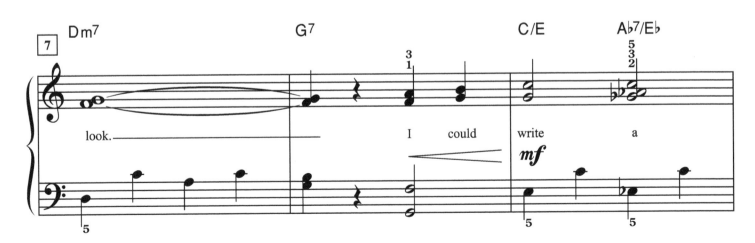

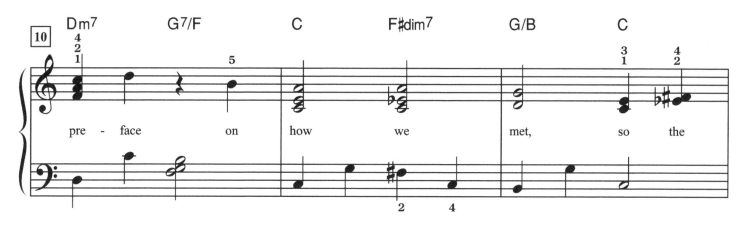

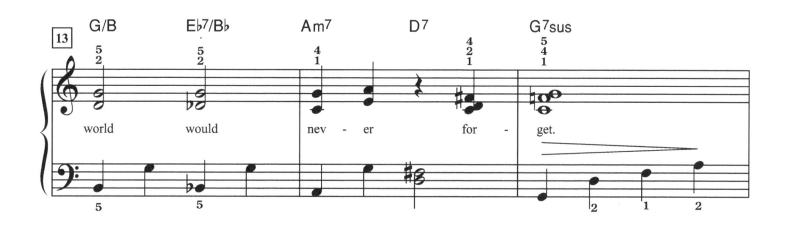

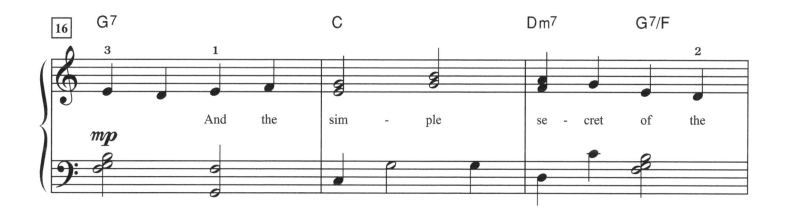

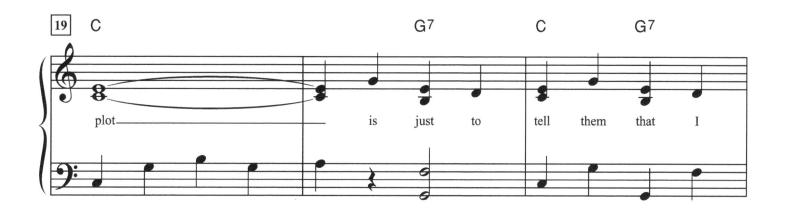

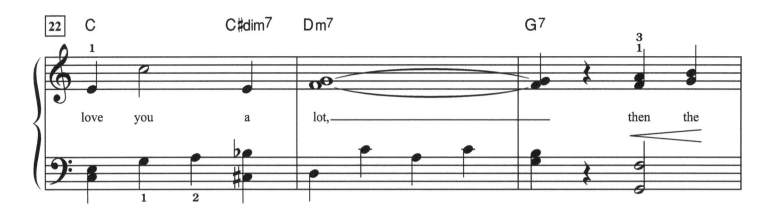

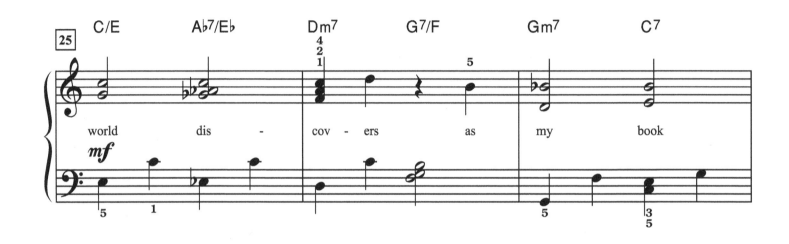

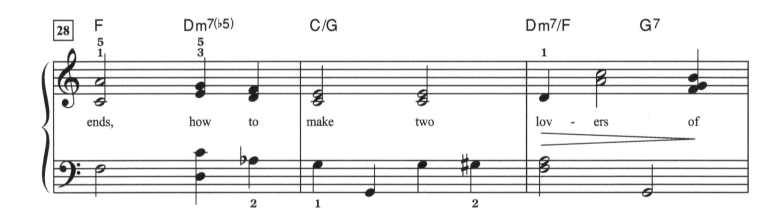

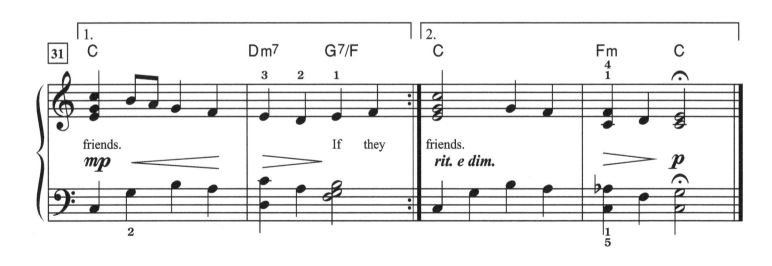

I GOT RHYTHM

Music and Lyrics by
George Gershwin and Ira Gershwin
Arranged by Dan Coates

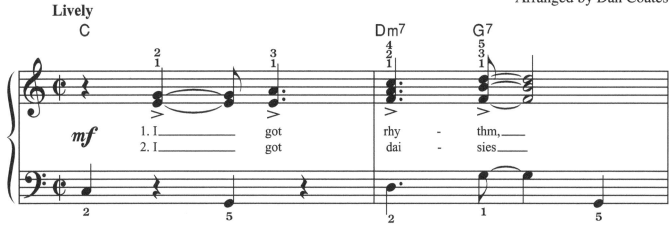

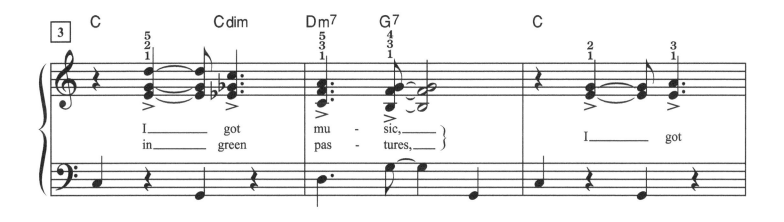

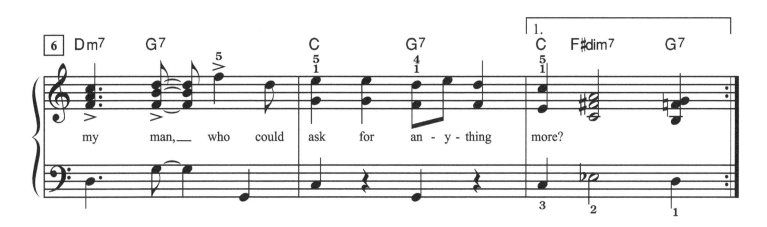

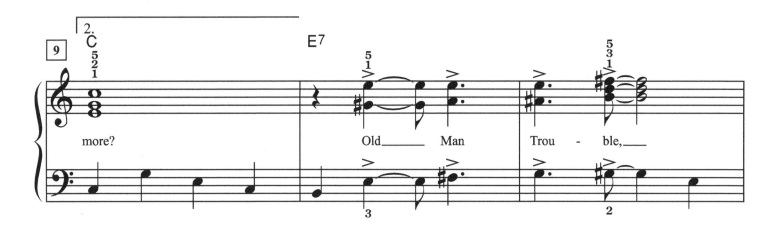

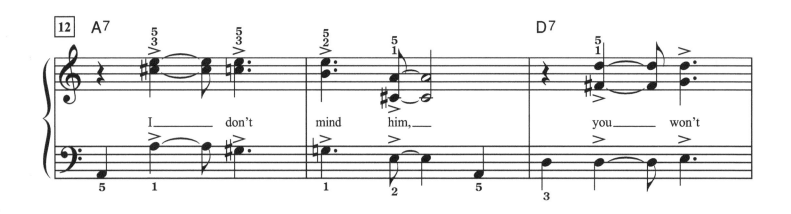

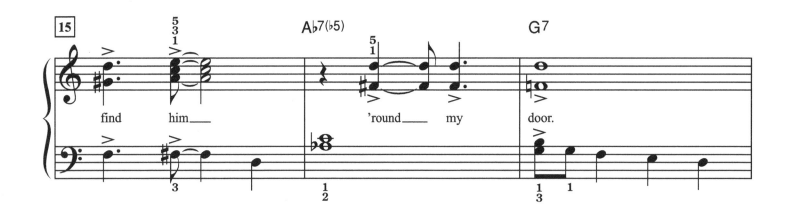

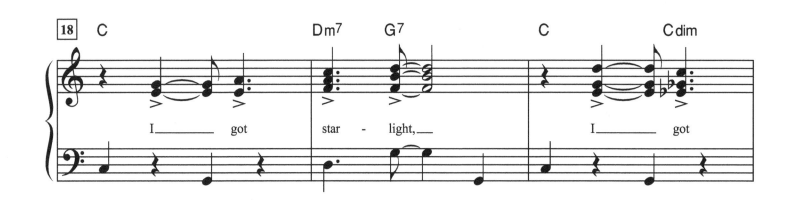

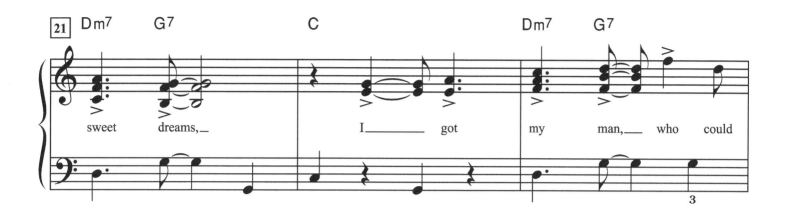

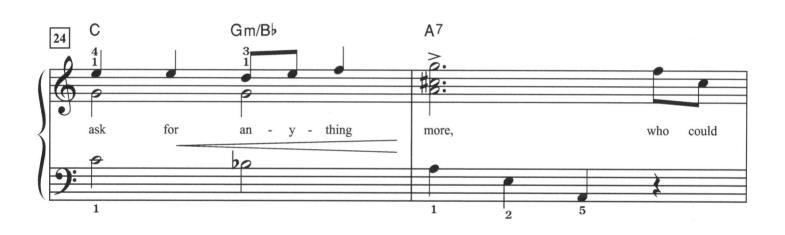

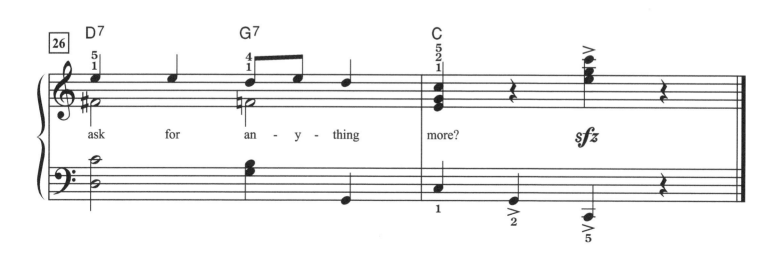

I LOVE PARIS

(from "Can-Can")

Words and Music by Cole Porter
Arranged by Dan Coates

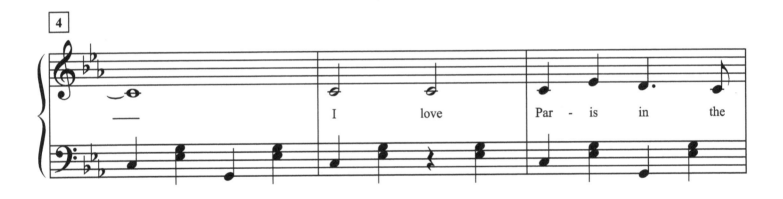

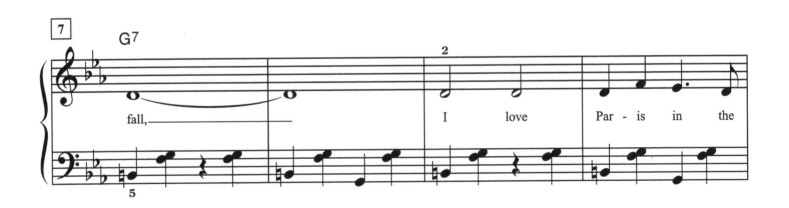

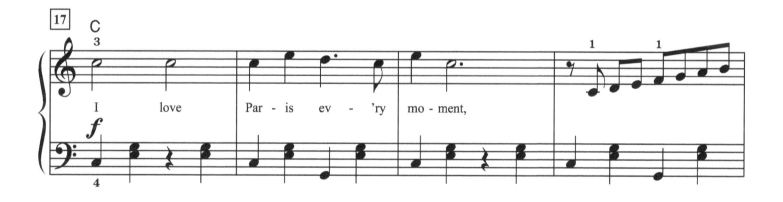

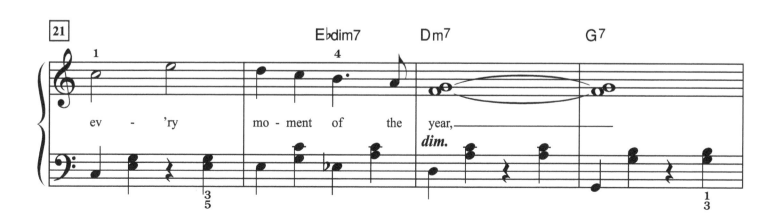

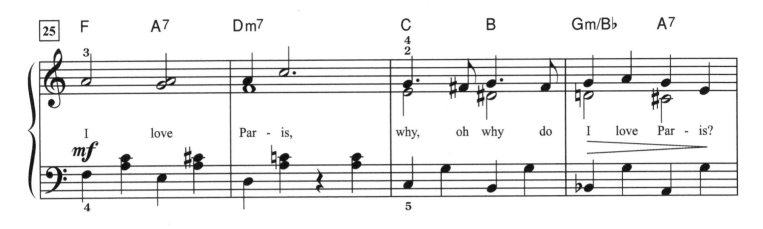

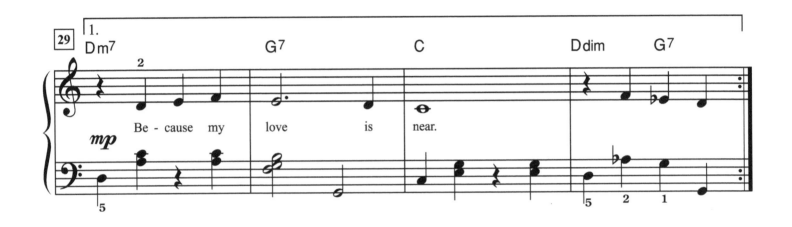

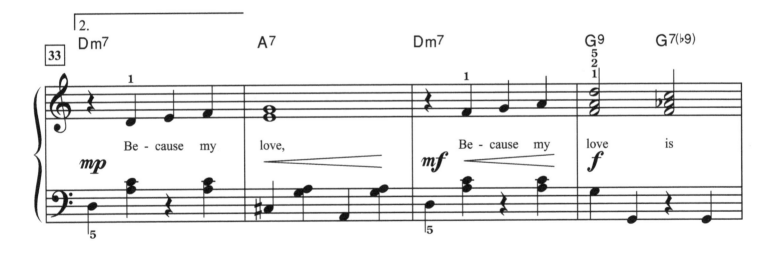

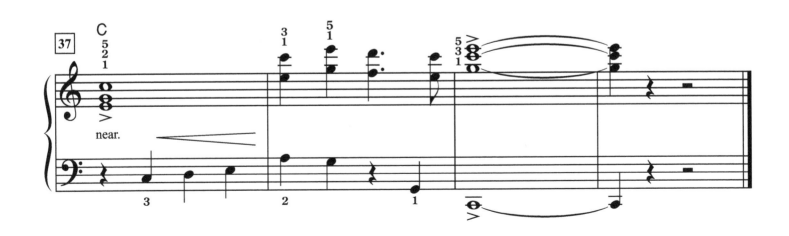

IN THE STILL OF THE NIGHT

(from "Rosalie")

Words and Music by Cole Porter
Arranged by Dan Coates

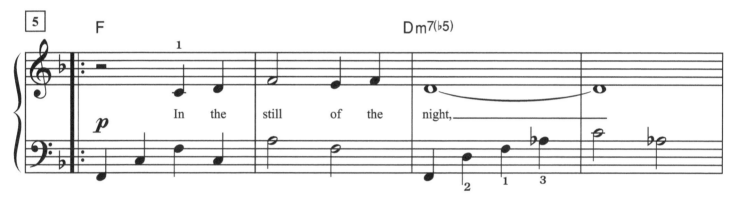

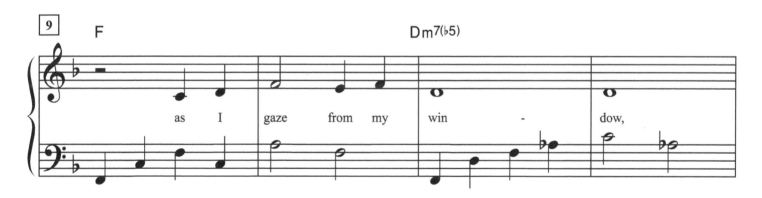

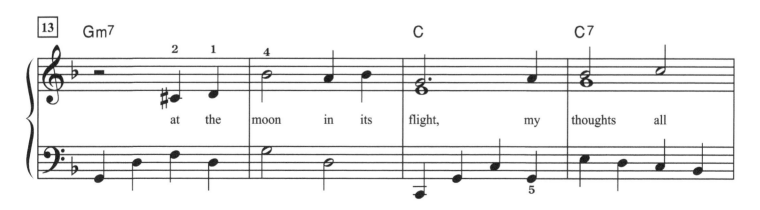

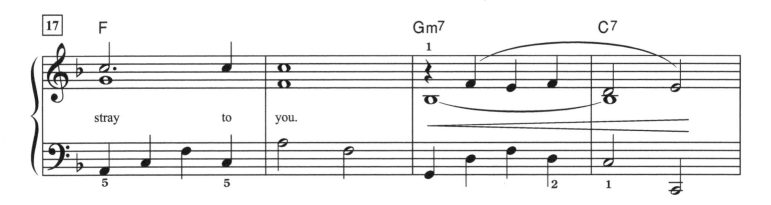

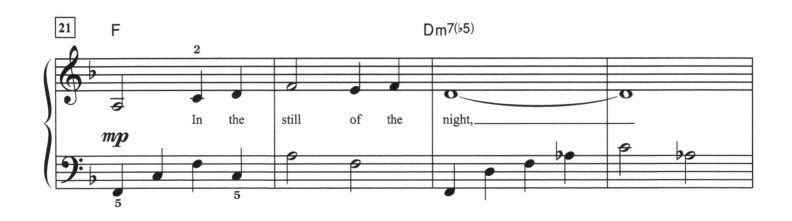

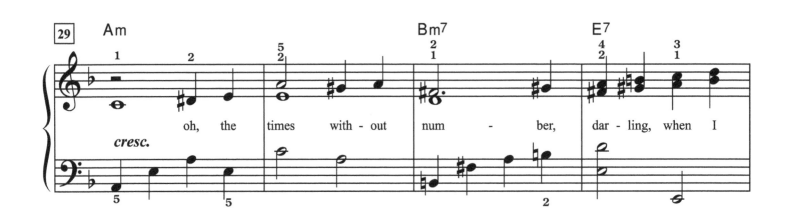

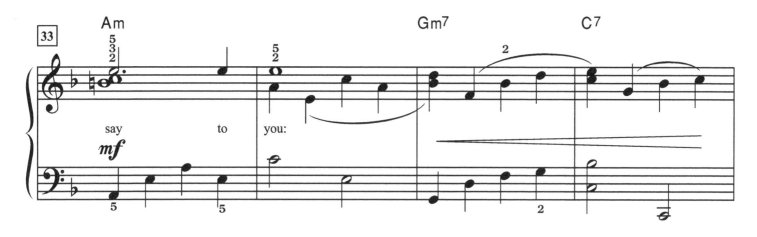

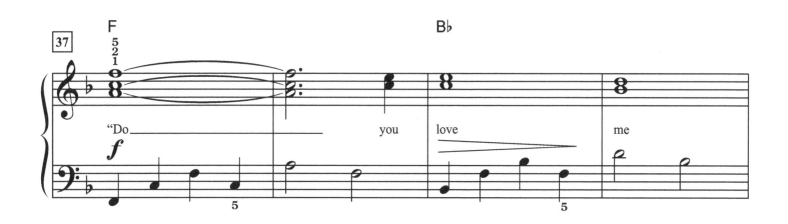

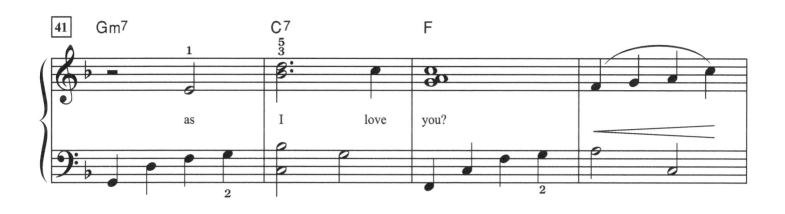

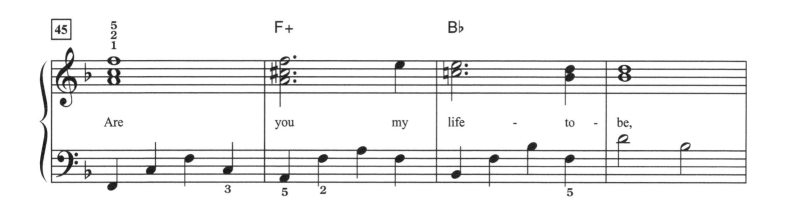

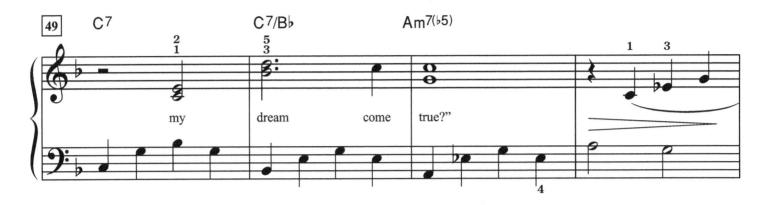

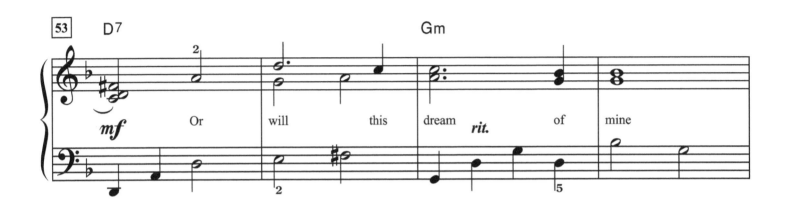

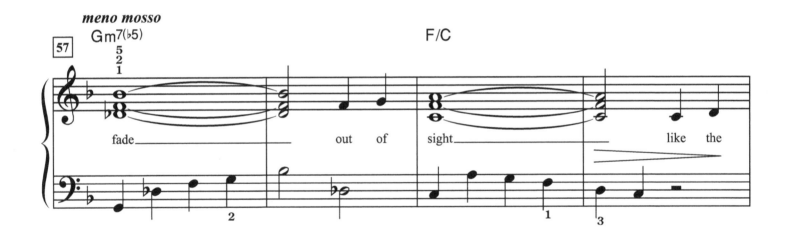

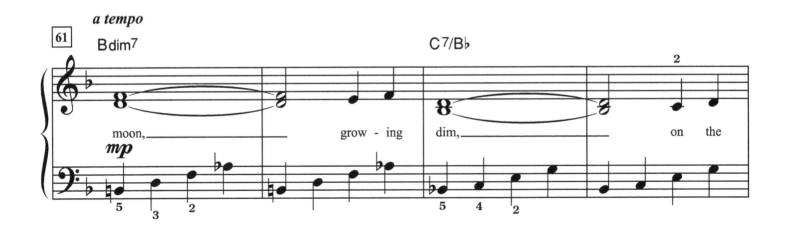

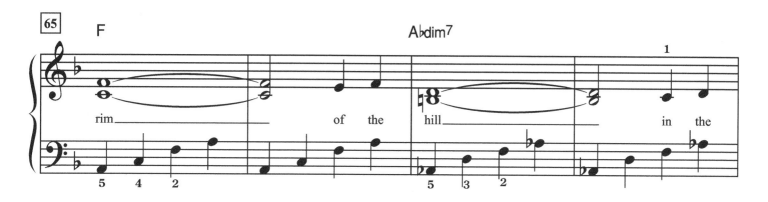

rim_____ of the hill_____ in the

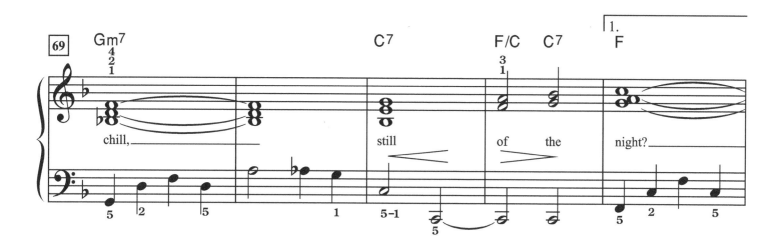

chill,_____ still of the night?_____

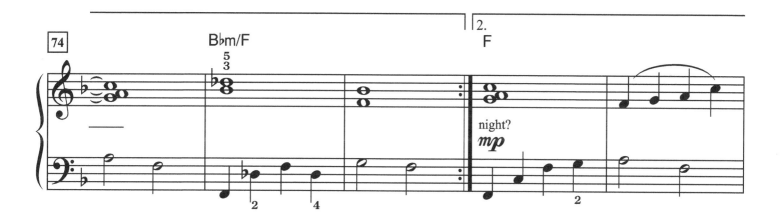

night?
mp

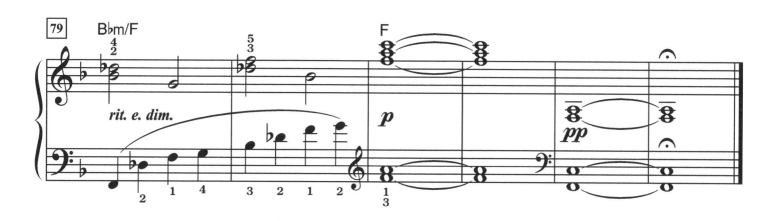

rit. e. dim. *p* *pp*

IT WAS A VERY GOOD YEAR

Words and Music by Ervin Drake
Arranged by Dan Coates

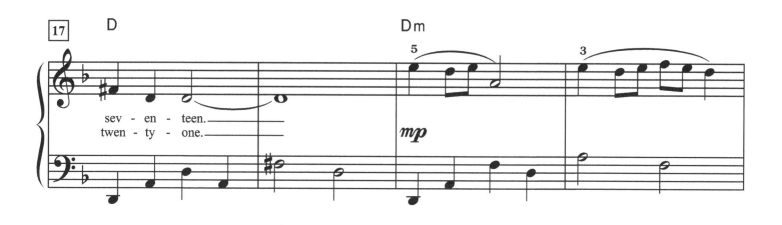

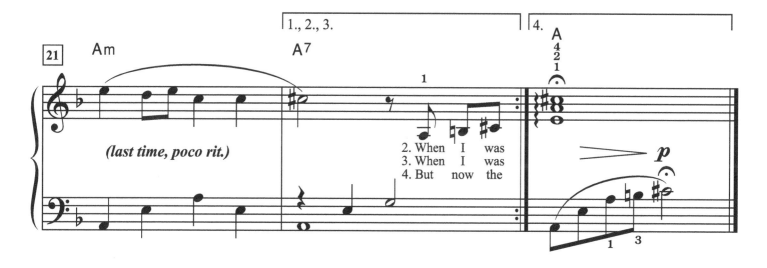

Verse 3:
When I was thirty-five, it was a very good year,
It was a very good year for blue-blooded girls of independent means.
We'd ride in limousines their chauffeurs would drive
When I was thirty-five.

Verse 4:
But now the days are short, I'm in the autumn of the year,
And now I think of my life as vintage wine from the old kegs.
From the brim to the dregs it poured sweet and clear;
It was a very good year.

IT'S DE-LOVELY

(from "Red, Hot & Blue")

Words and Music by Cole Porter
Arranged by Dan Coates

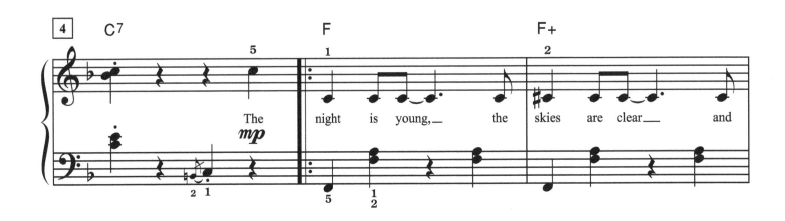

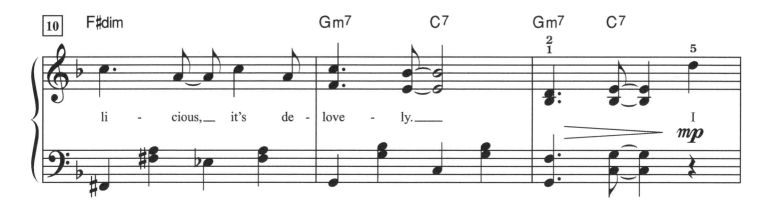

li - cious,__ it's de - love - ly.__ *mp*

un - der - stand__ the reas - on why__ you're sent - i - ment - al, 'cause

cresc.

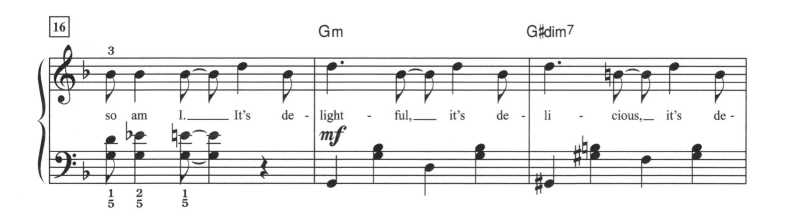

so am I.____ It's de - light - ful,__ it's de - li - cious,__ it's de -

mf

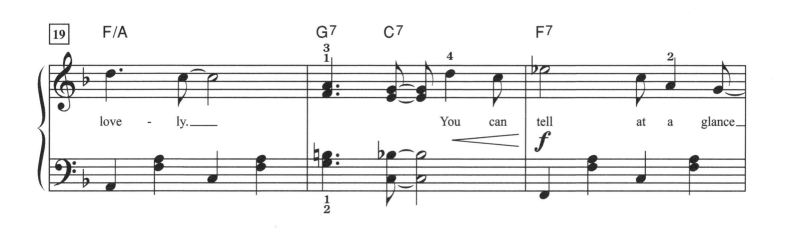

love - ly.____ You can tell at a glance__

f

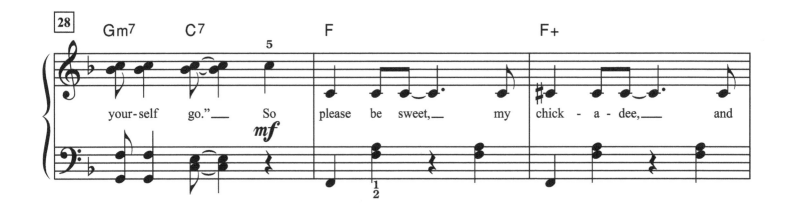

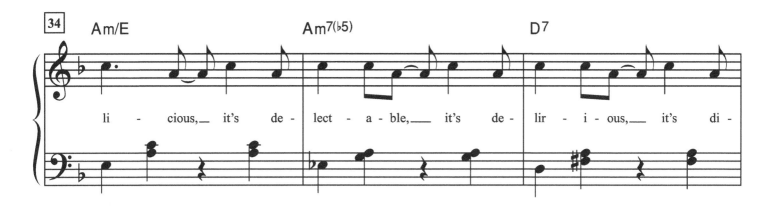

I'VE GOT YOU UNDER MY SKIN

(from "Born to Dance")

Words and Music by Cole Porter
Arranged by Dan Coates

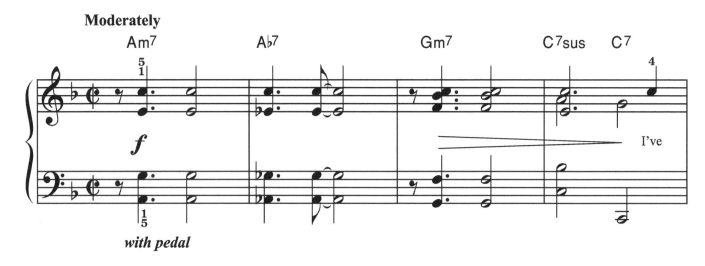

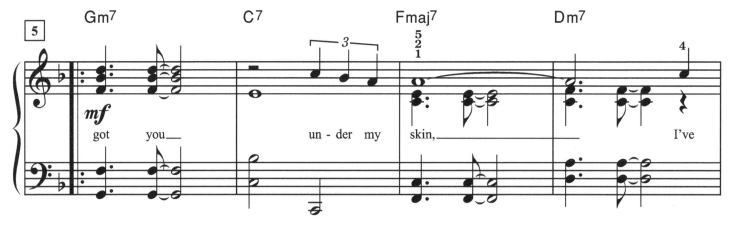

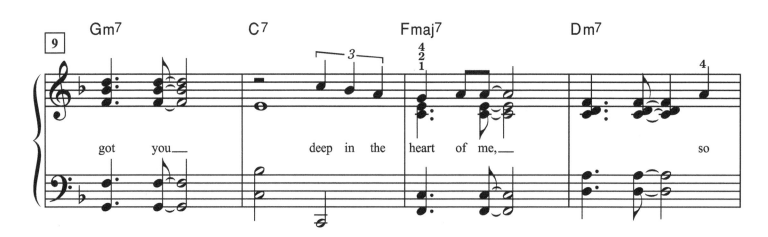

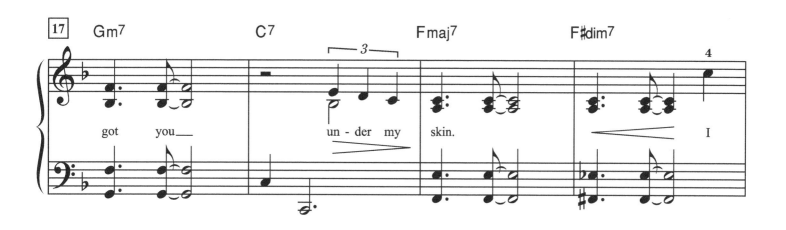

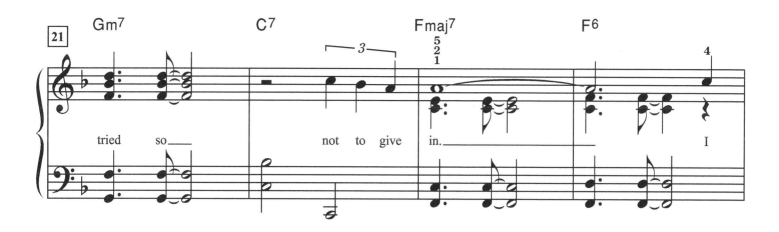

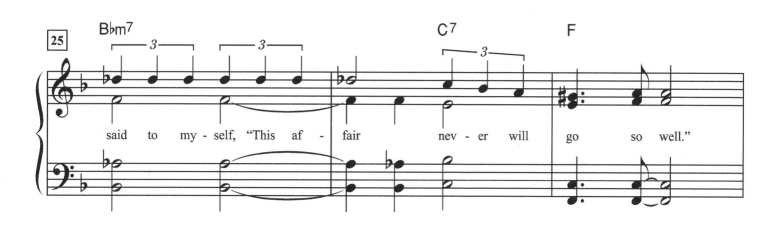

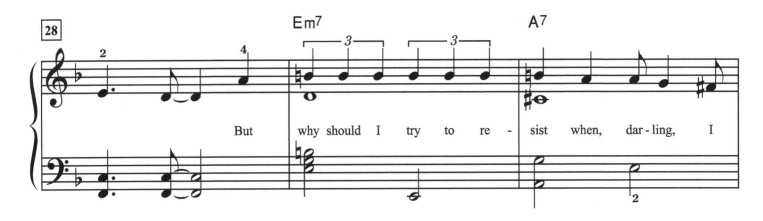

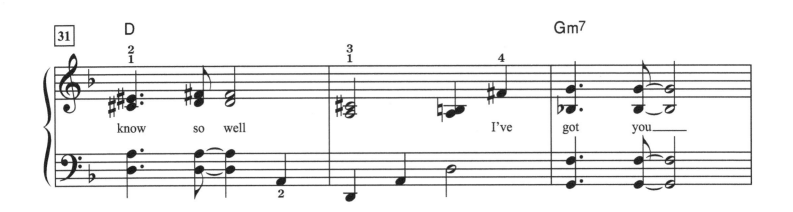

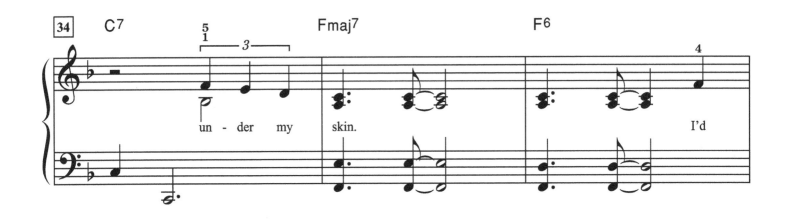

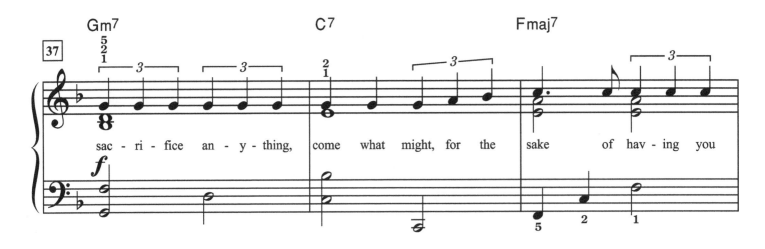

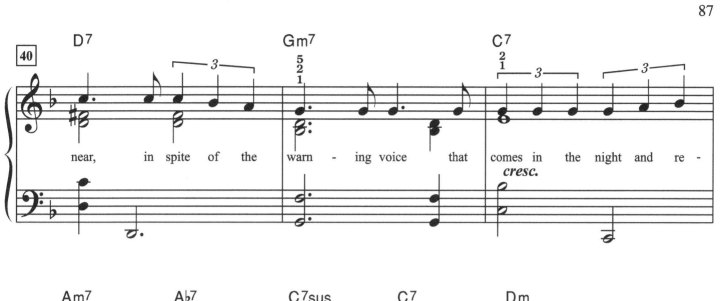

near, in spite of the warn - ing voice that comes in the night and re -

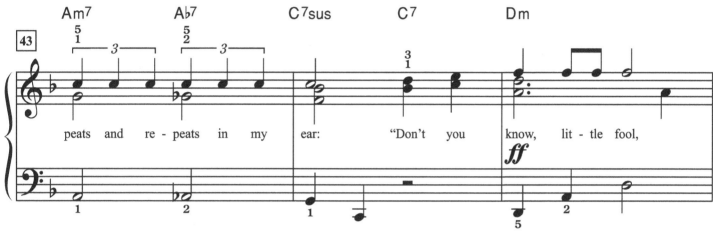

peats and re - peats in my ear: "Don't you know, lit - tle fool,

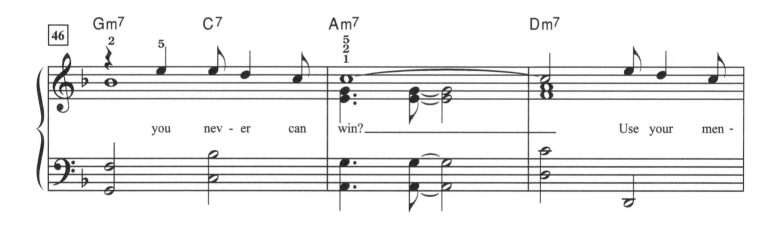

you nev - er can win?_____ Use your men -

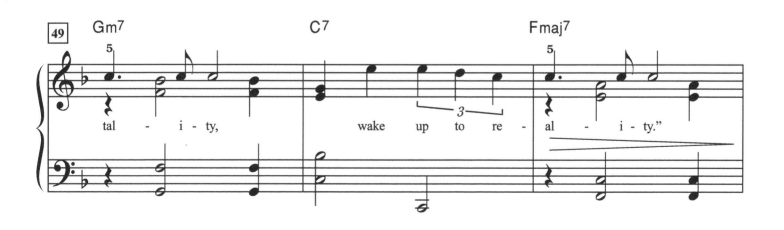

tal - i - ty, wake up to re - al - i - ty."

But each time I do,___ just the thought of you___ makes me

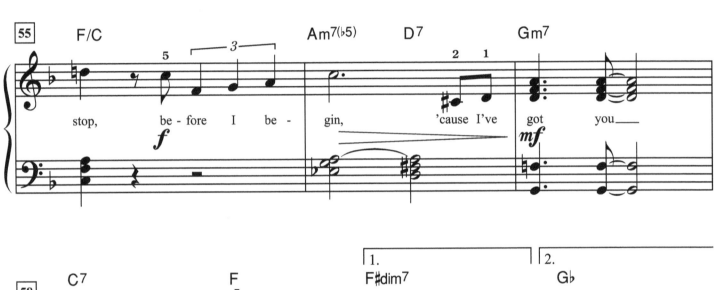

stop, be - fore I be - gin, 'cause I've got you___

un - der my skin. I've

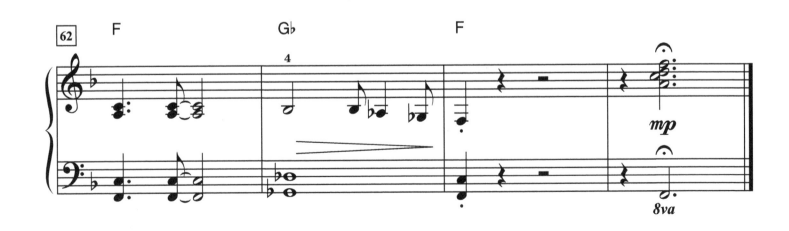

JUST ONE OF THOSE THINGS

(from "High Society")

Words and Music by Cole Porter
Arranged by Dan Coates

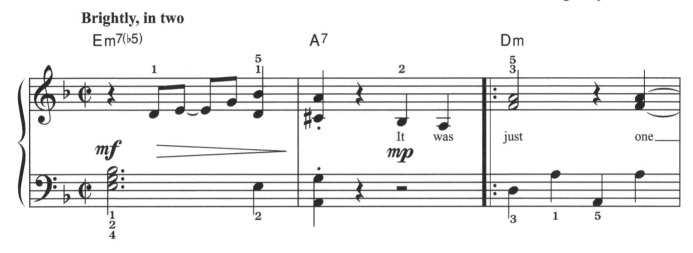

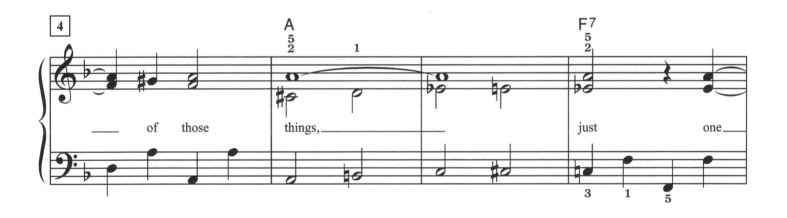

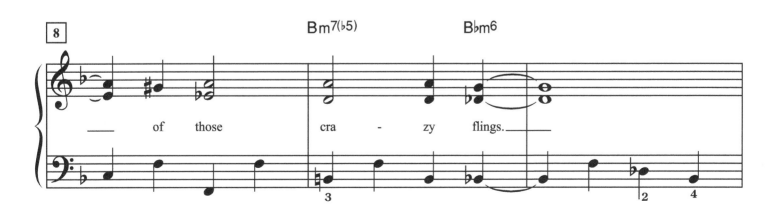

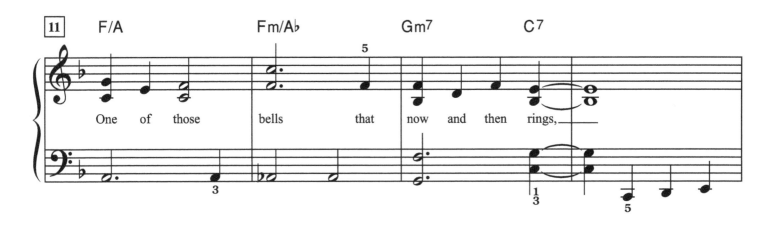

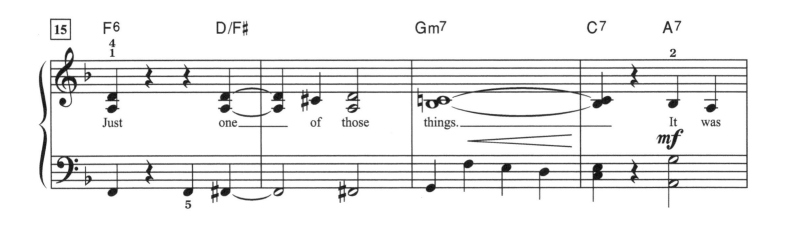

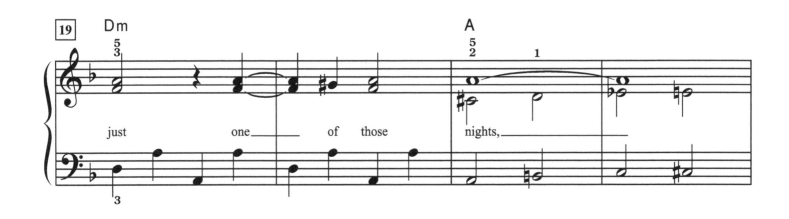

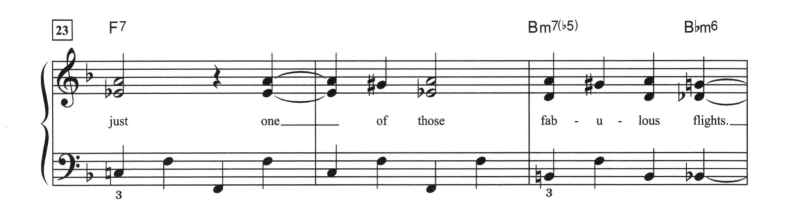

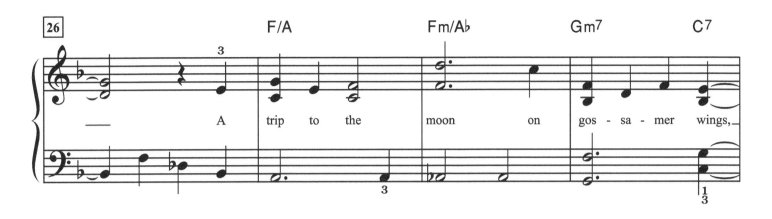

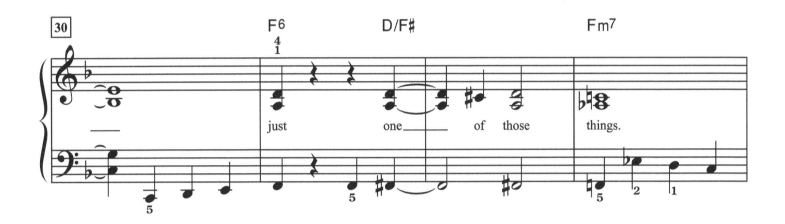

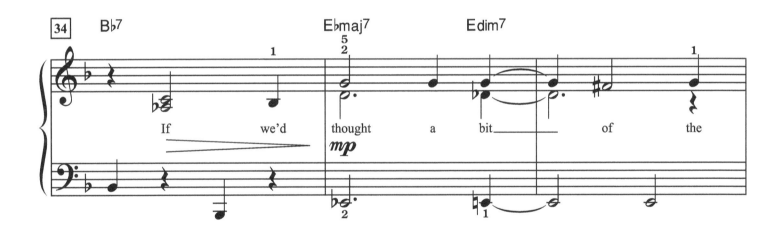

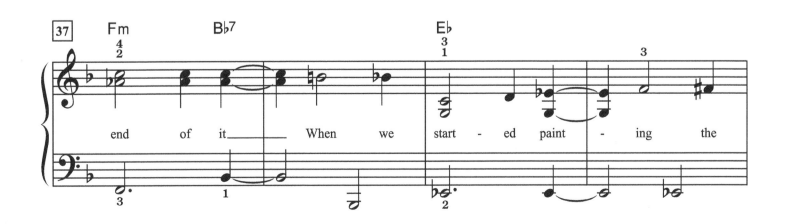

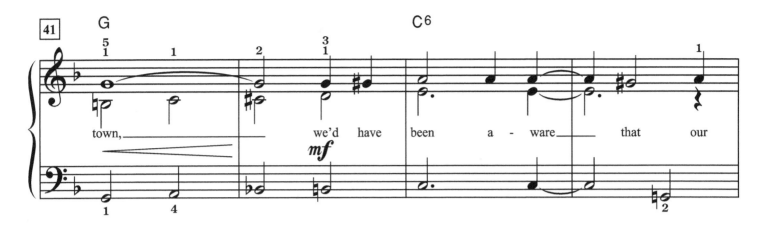

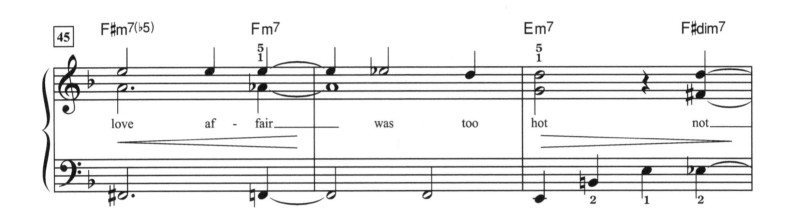

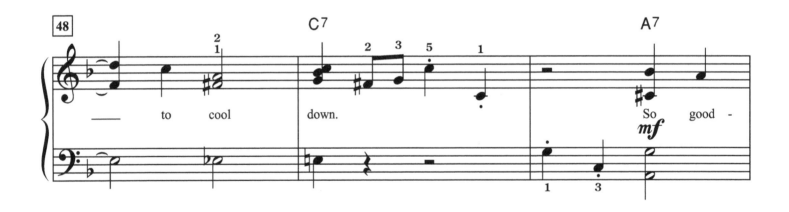

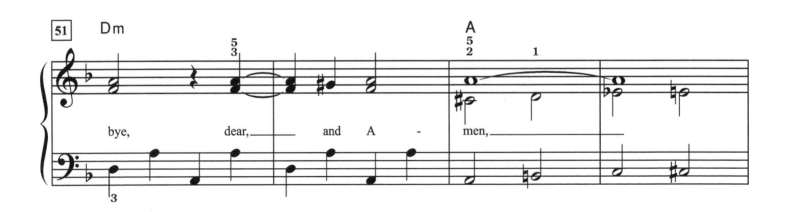

here's hop - ing we meet now and then,

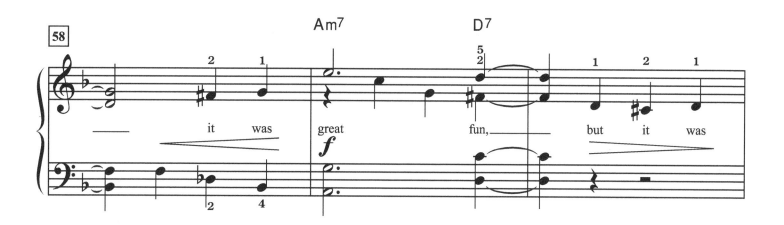

it was great fun, but it was

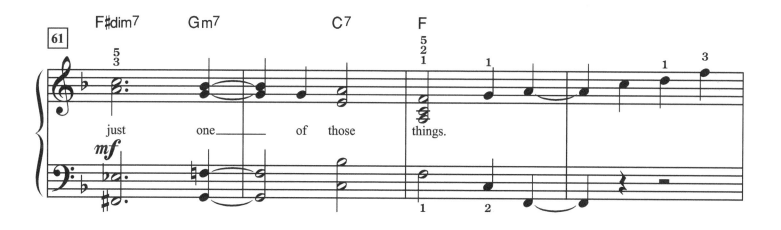

just one of those things.

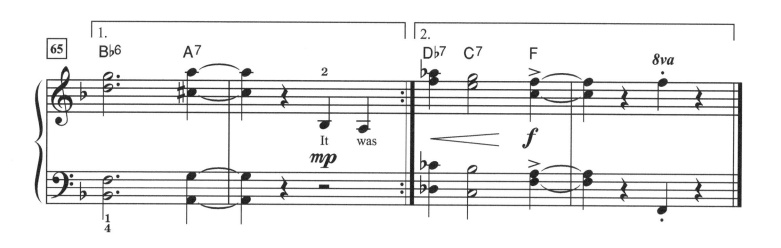

It was

THE LADY IS A TRAMP

(from "Babes In Arms")

Words by Lorenz Hart
Music by Richard Rodgers
Arranged by Dan Coates

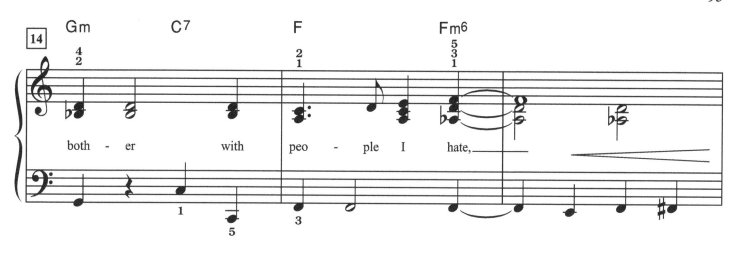

both - er with peo - ple I hate,_____

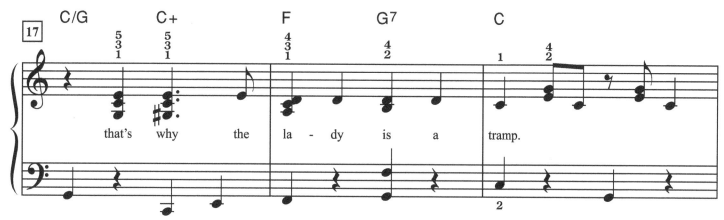

that's why the la - dy is a tramp.

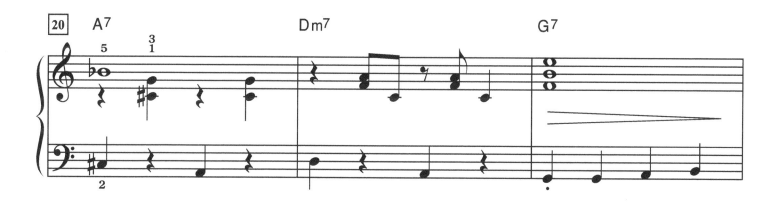

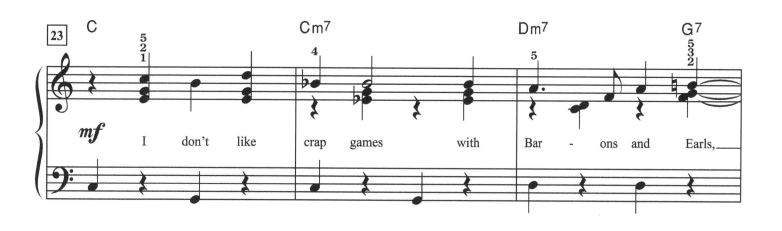

mf I don't like crap games with Bar - ons and Earls,_____

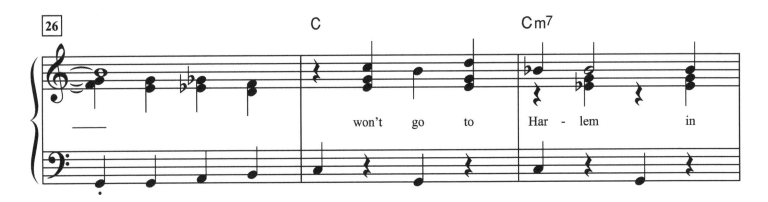

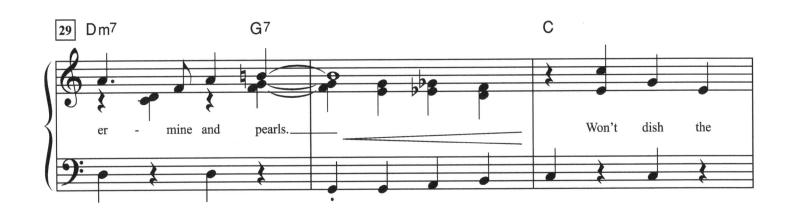

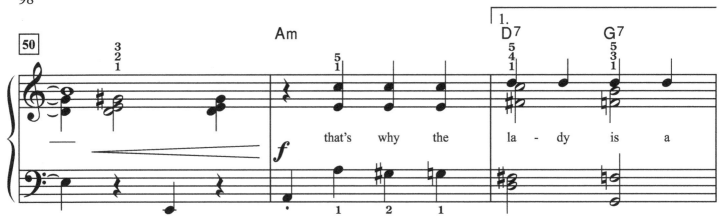

that's why the la - dy is a

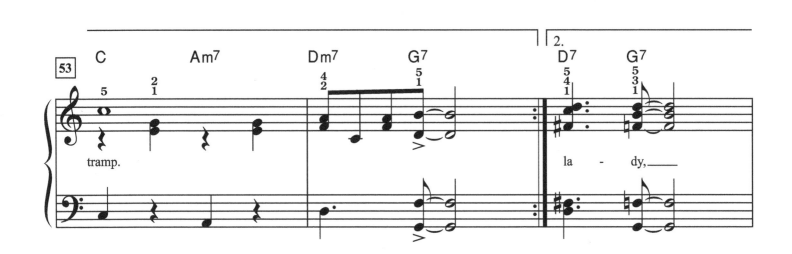

tramp.

la - dy,

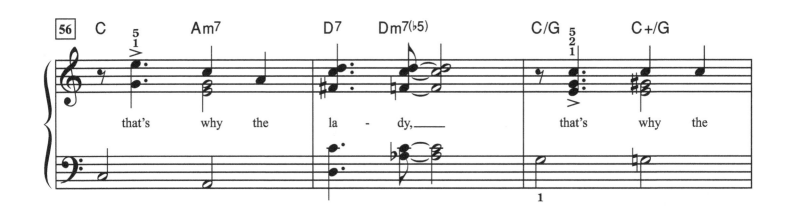

that's why the la - dy, that's why the

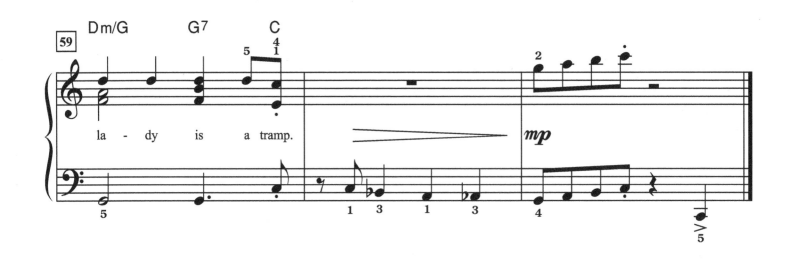

la - dy is a tramp.

LET'S CALL THE WHOLE THING OFF

(from "Shall We Dance")

Music and Lyrics by
George Gershwin and Ira Gershwin
Arranged by Dan Coates

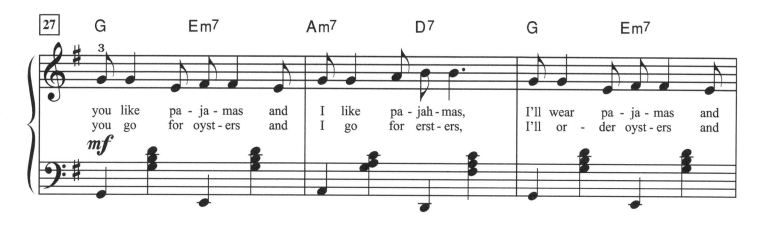

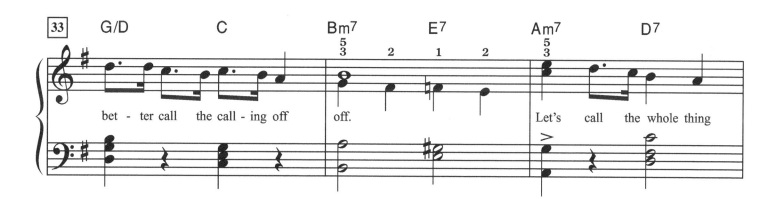

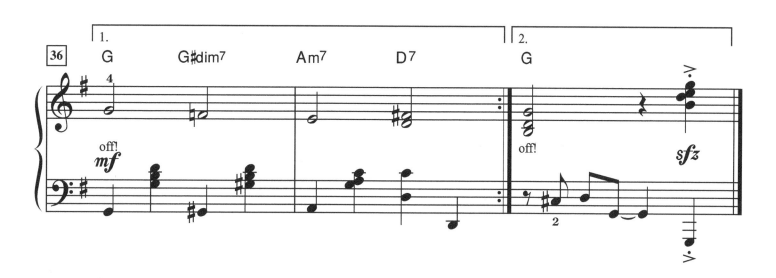

MACK THE KNIFE

Words by Marc Blitzstein
Music by Kurt Weill
Arranged by Dan Coates

Moderately, with a steady beat

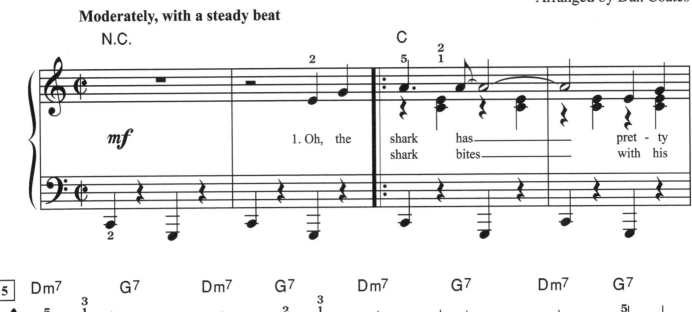

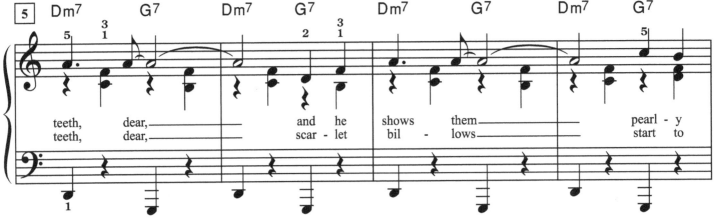

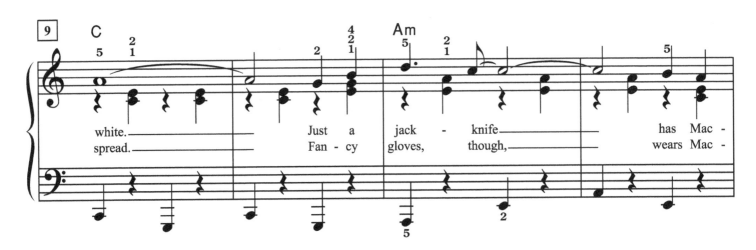

104

MAKIN' WHOOPEE

(from "Whoopee")

Lyrics by Gus Kahn
Music by Walter Donaldson
Arranged by Dan Coates

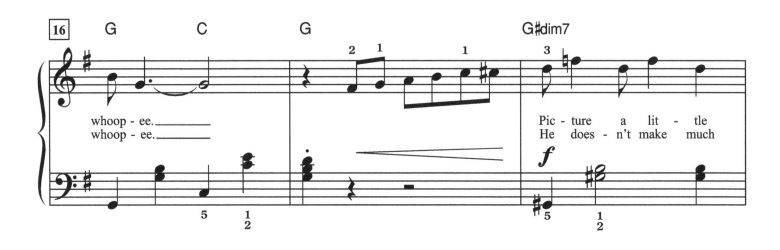

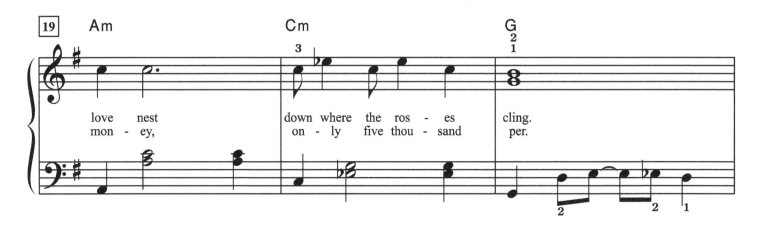

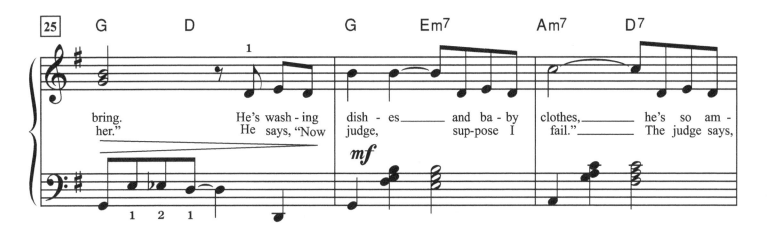

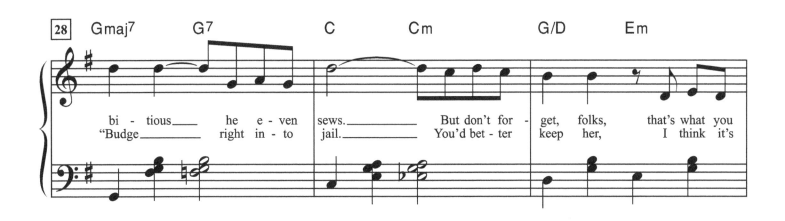

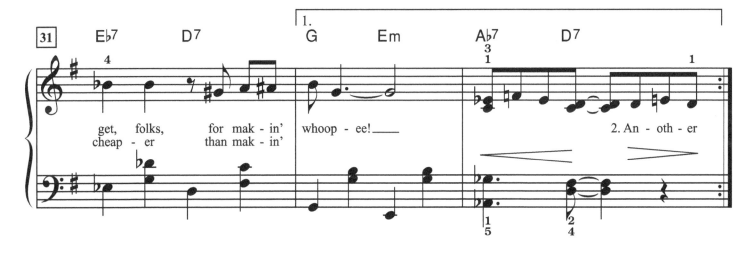

THE MAN THAT GOT AWAY

(from "A Star is Born")

Words by Ira Gershwin
Music by Harold Arlen
Arranged by Dan Coates

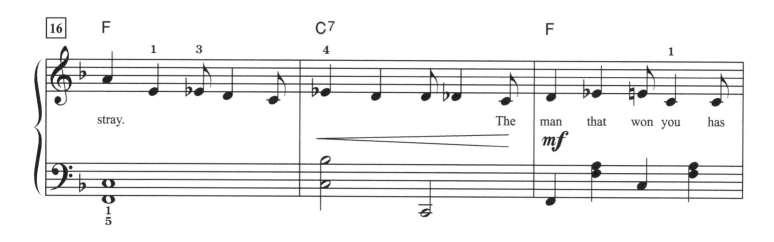

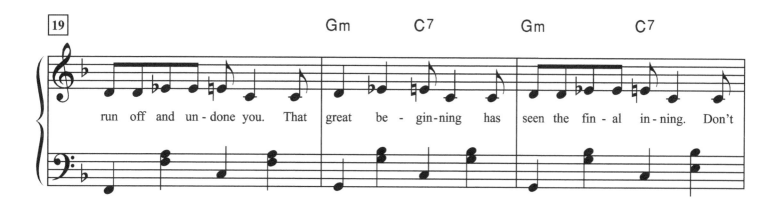

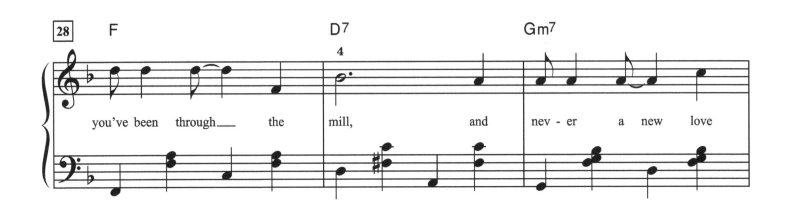

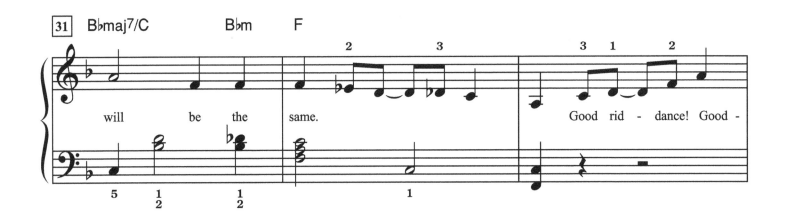

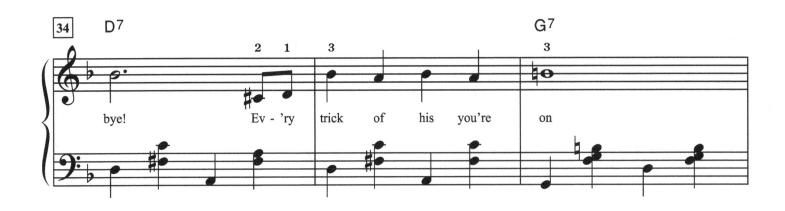

to. But fools will be fools, and where's he

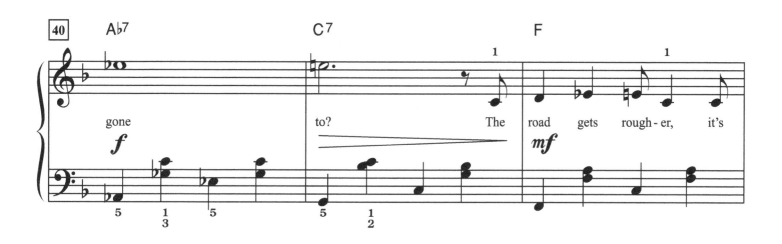

gone to? The road gets rough-er, it's

lone-li-er and tough-er, with hope you burn up, to-mor-row he may turn up. There's

just no let-up the live-long night and day!

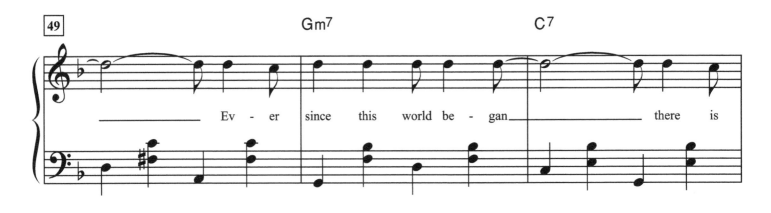

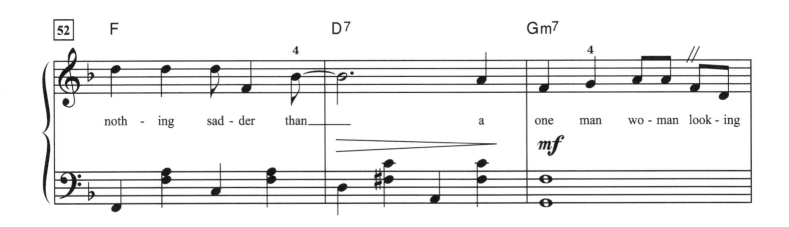

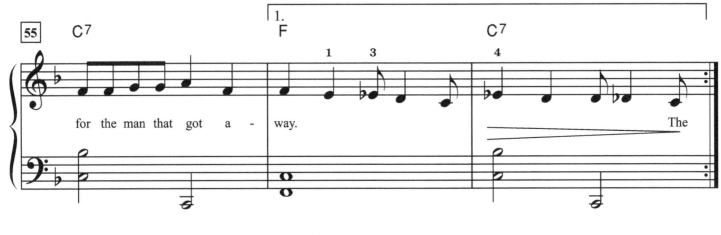

MISTY

Words by Johnny Burke
Music by Erroll Garner
Arranged by Dan Coates

Slowly, with expression

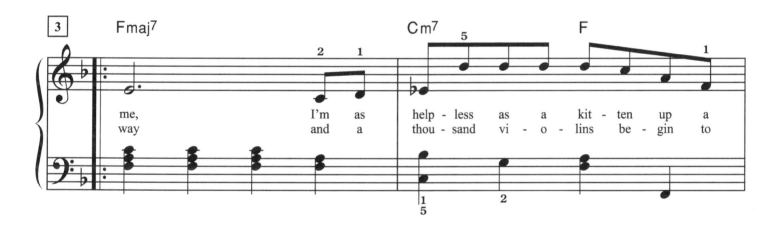

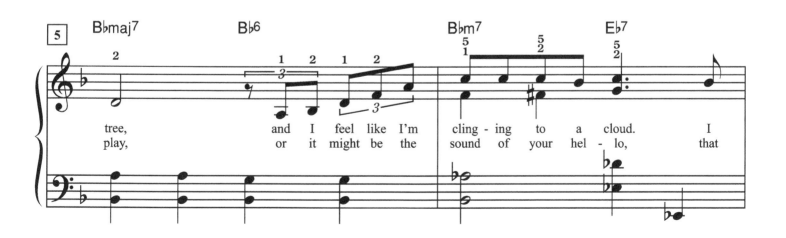

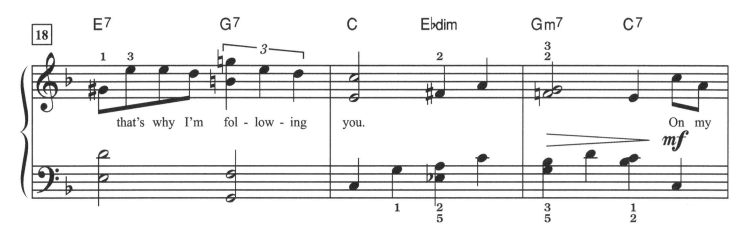

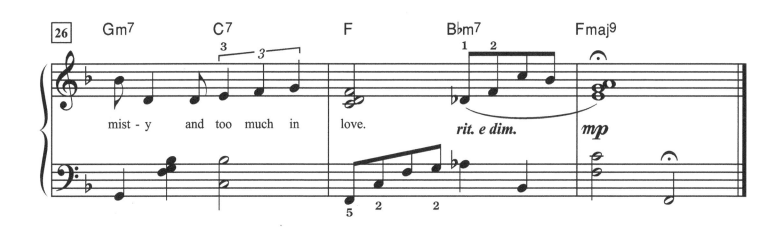

MOONDANCE

Words and Music by Van Morrison
Arranged by Dan Coates

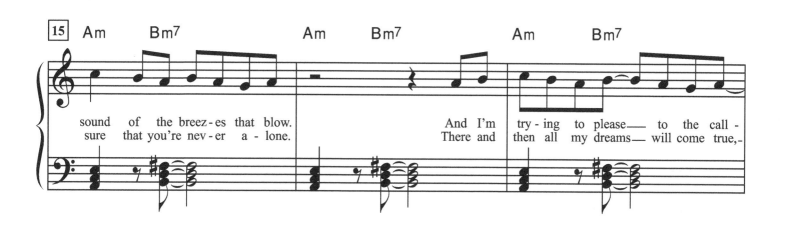

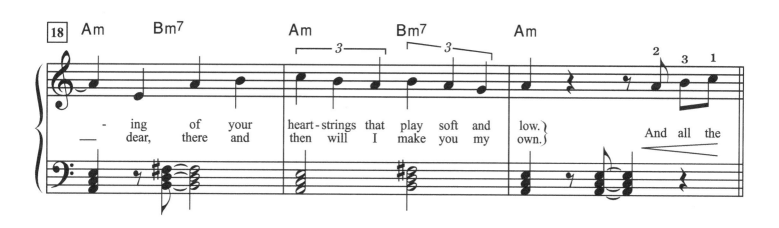

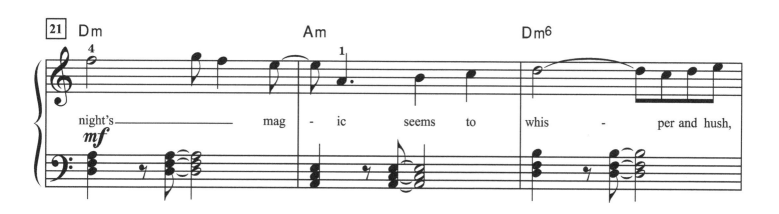

MOONLIGHT IN VERMONT

Music by Karl Suessdorf
Lyric by John Blackburn
Arranged by Dan Coates

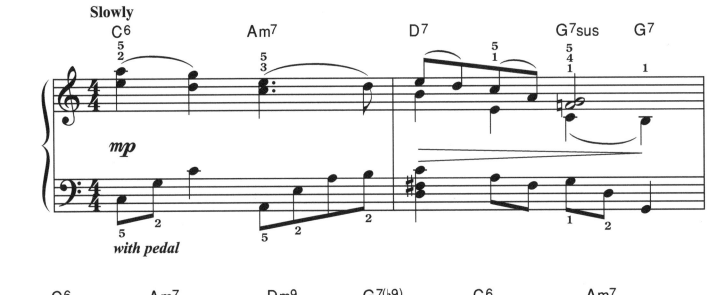

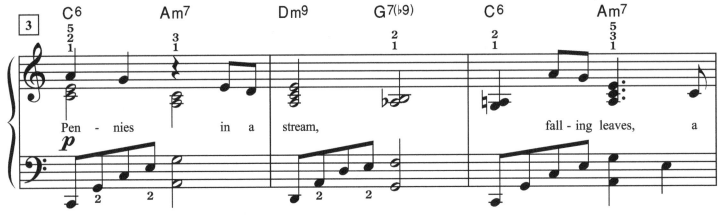

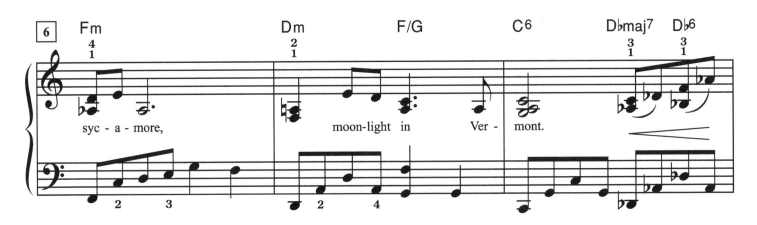

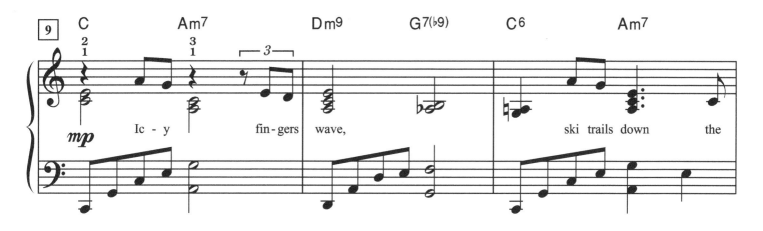

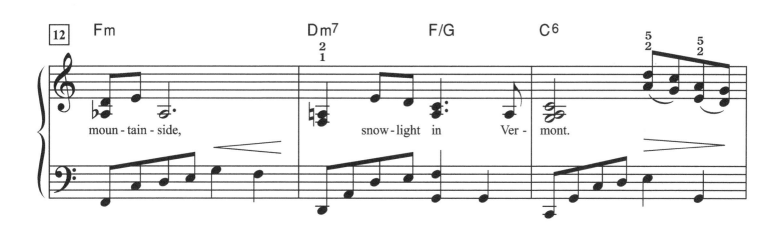

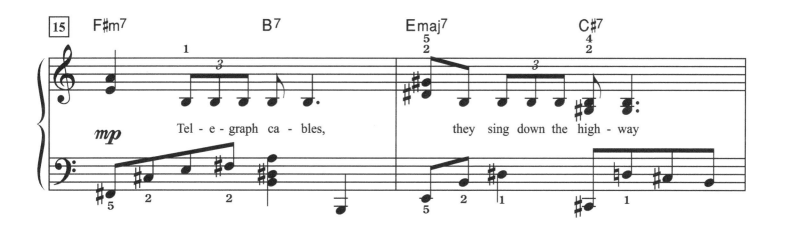

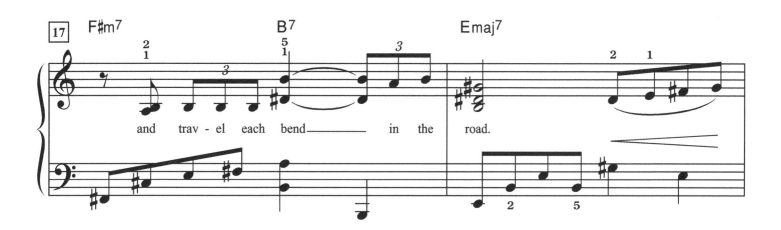

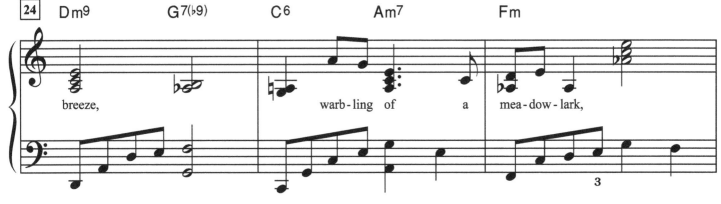

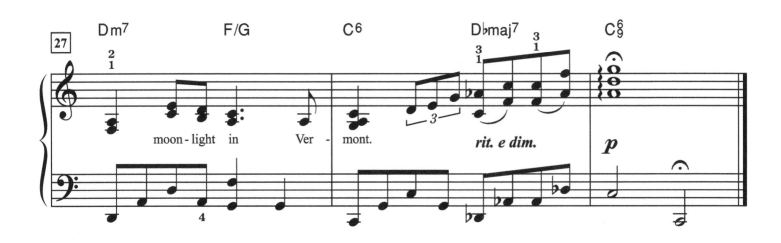

MY FUNNY VALENTINE

(from "Babes in Arms")

Words by Lorenz Hart
Music by Richard Rodgers
Arranged by Dan Coates

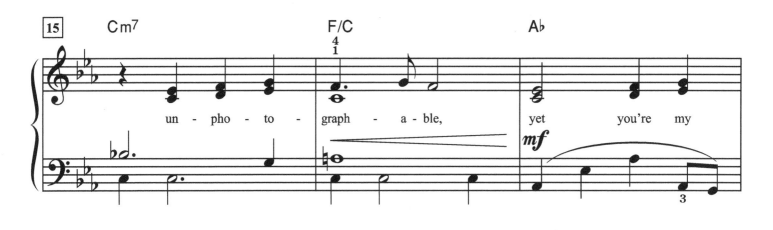

un - pho - to - graph - a - ble, yet you're my

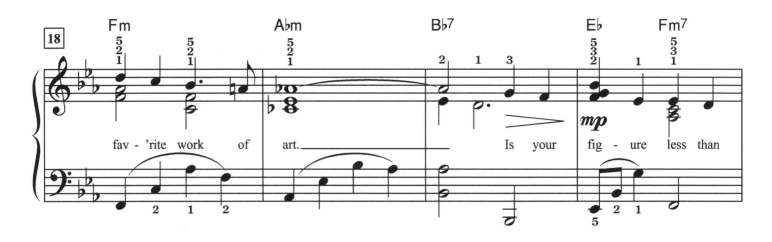

fav - 'rite work of art. Is your fig - ure less than

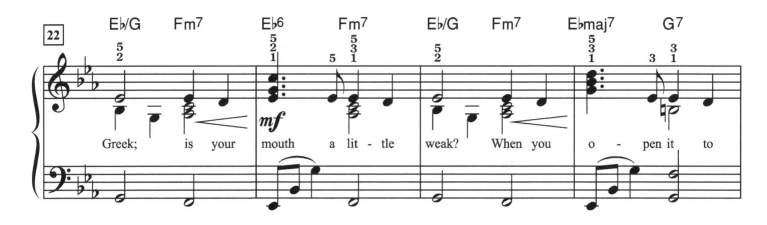

Greek; is your mouth a lit - tle weak? When you o - pen it to

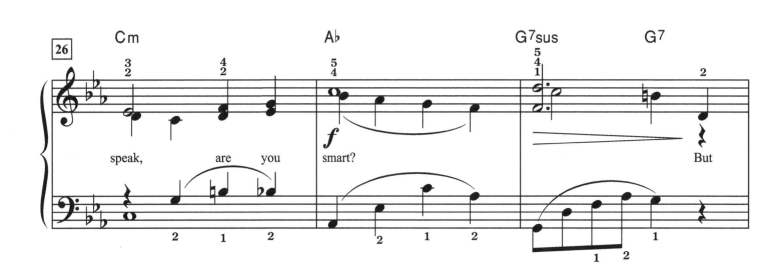

speak, are you smart? But

29
Cm
G/C
Cm7
don't change a hair for me, not if you
mp
32
F7
A♭
D7(♭5)
G7
care for me. Stay, lit - tle Val - en - tine,
mf
35
Cm
E♭7
A♭
Fm7
B♭7
stay!
Each day is Val - en - tine's
39
1.
E♭
G7(♯5)
G7
2.
E♭
8va
day.
day.
rit.
p

NIGHT AND DAY

(from "The Gay Divorcee")

Words and Music by Cole Porter
Arranged by Dan Coates

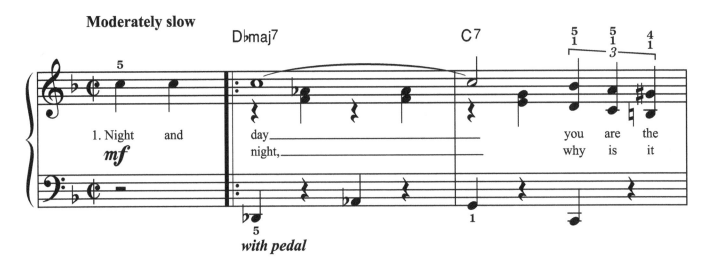

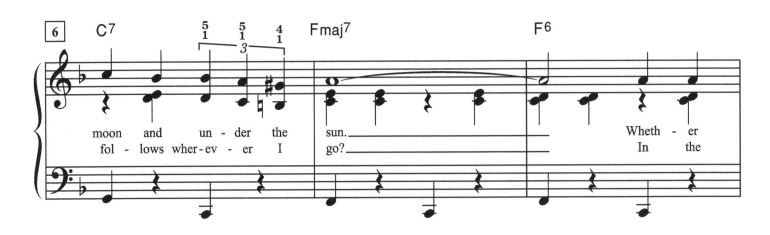

near to me or far, it's no mat - ter, dar - ling,
roar - ing traf - fic's boom, in the si - lence of my

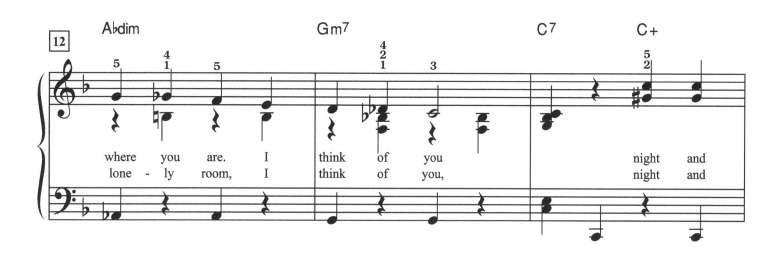

where you are. I think of you night and
lone - ly room, I think of you, night and

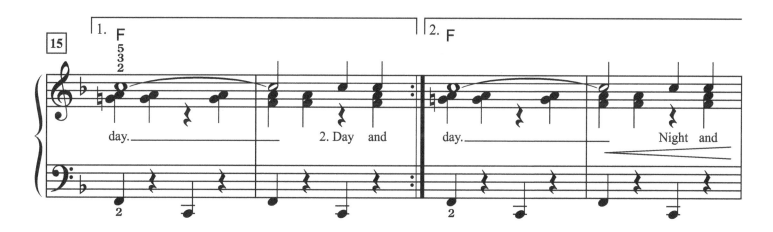

1. day._____ 2. Day and day._____ Night and

day_____ un - der the hide of me,_____

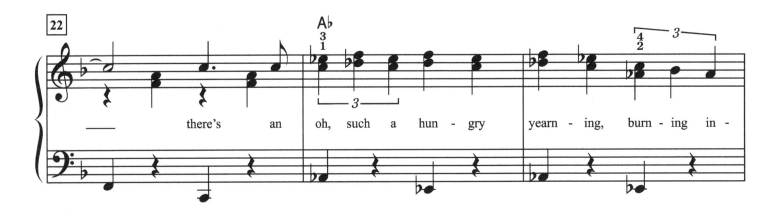

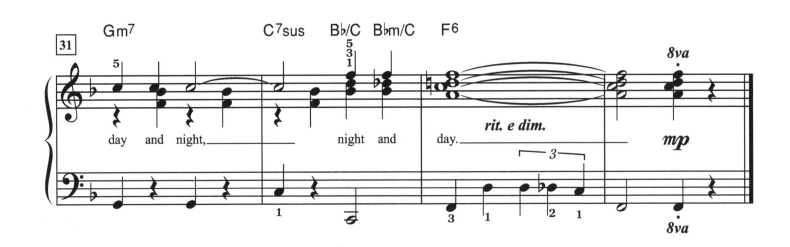

ON THE STREET WHERE YOU LIVE

(from "My Fair Lady")

Words by Alan Jay Lerner
Music by Frederick Loewe
Arranged by Dan Coates

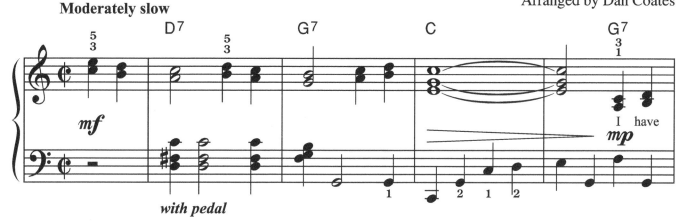

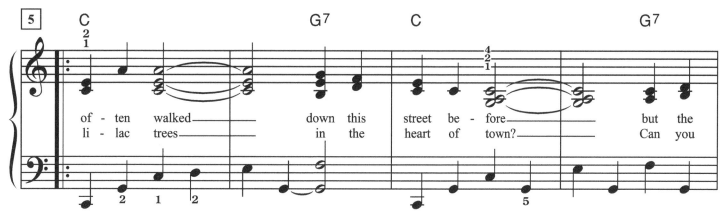

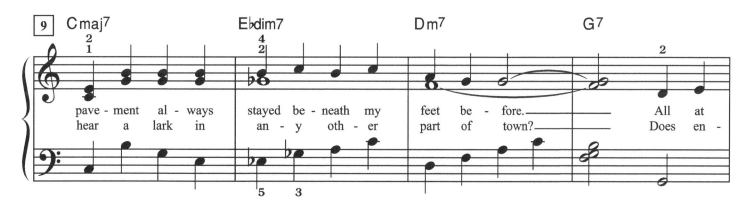

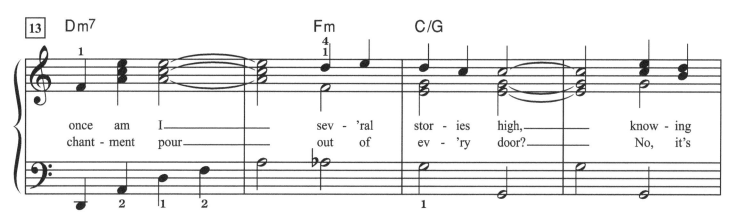

OVER THE RAINBOW

(from "The Wizard of Oz")

Music by Harold Arlen
Lyrics by E.Y. Harburg
Arranged by Dan Coates

Moderately, with expression

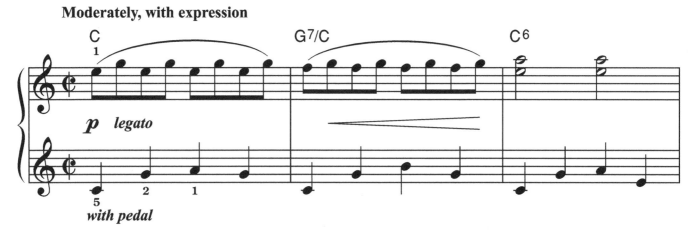

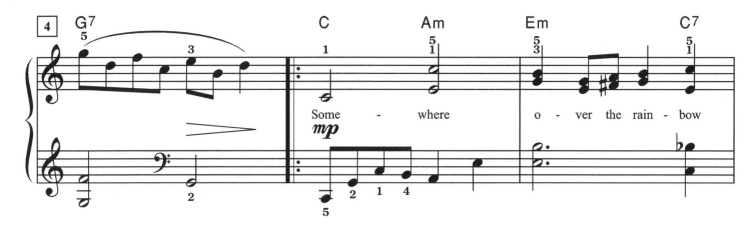

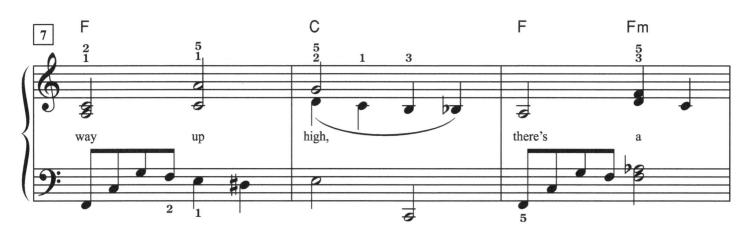

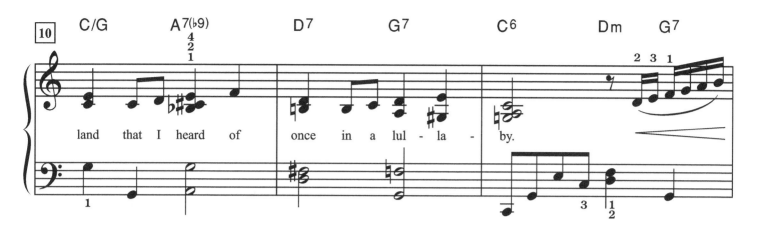

land that I heard of once in a lul - la - by.

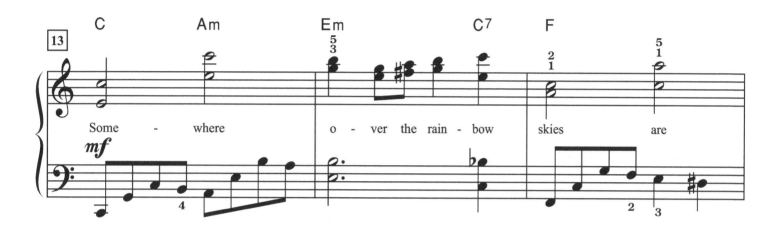

Some - where o - ver the rain - bow skies are

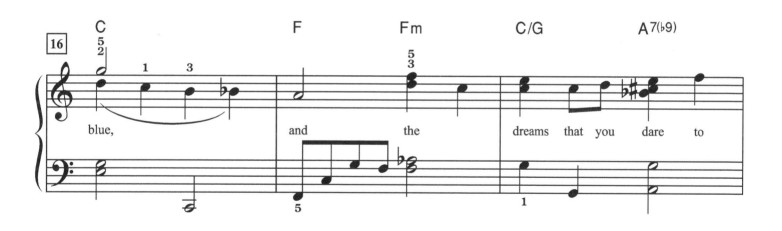

blue, and the dreams that you dare to

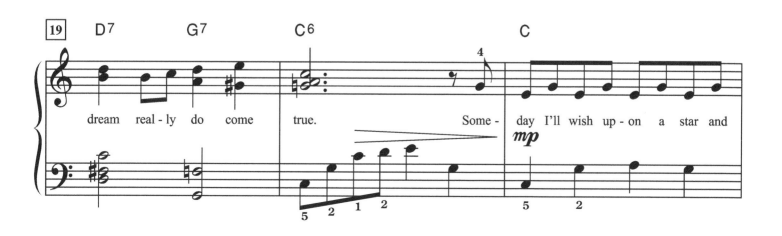

dream real - ly do come true. Some - day I'll wish up - on a star and

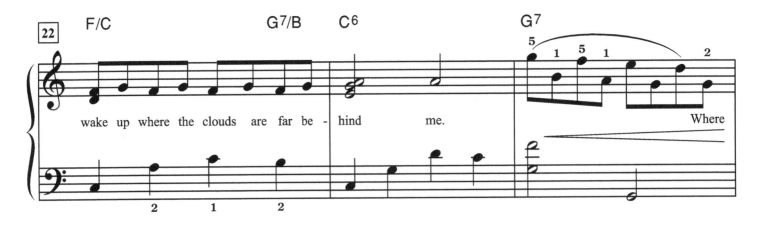

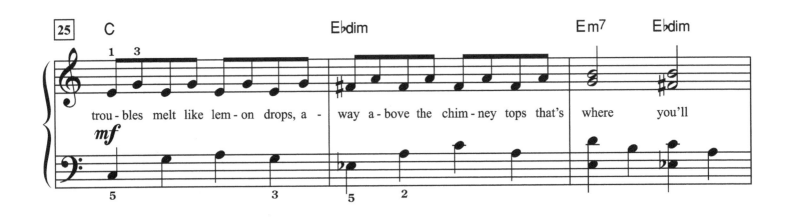

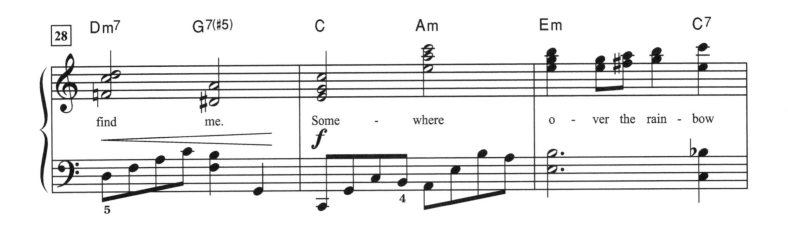

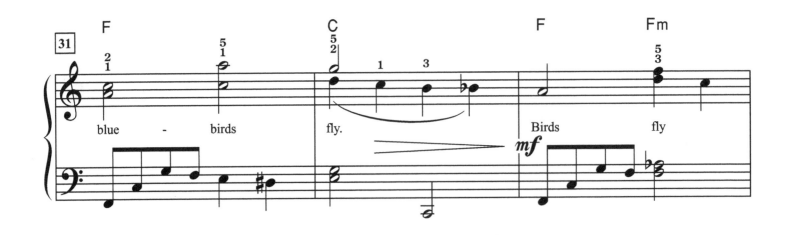

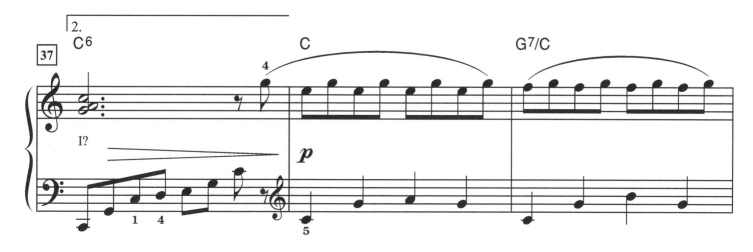

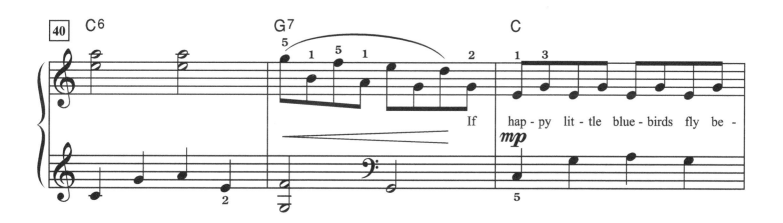

PETER GUNN

(from "Peter Gunn")

By Henry Mancini
Arranged by Dan Coates

THE PINK PANTHER

(from "The Pink Panther")

By Henry Mancini
Arranged by Dan Coates

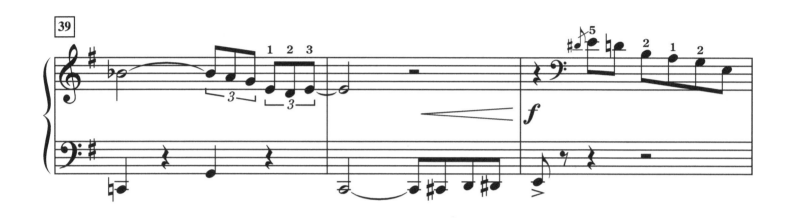

RAGS TO RICHES

Words and Music by
Richard Adler and Jerry Ross
Arranged by Dan Coates

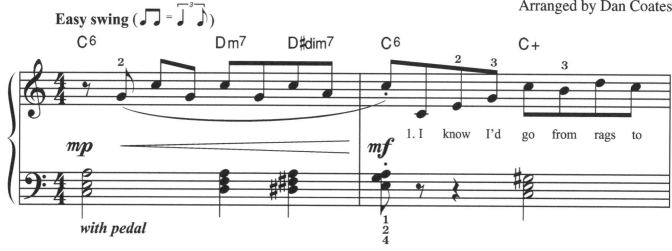

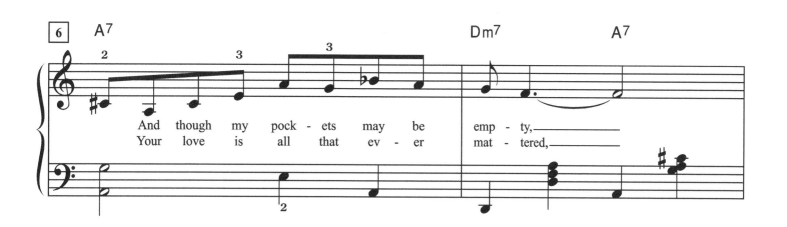

142

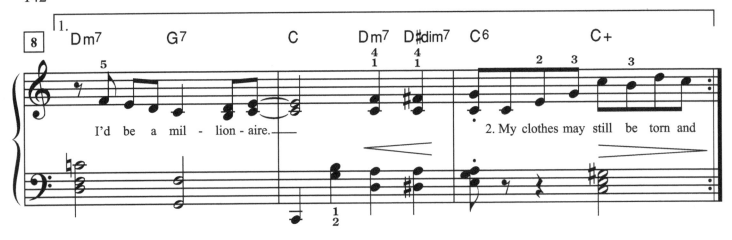

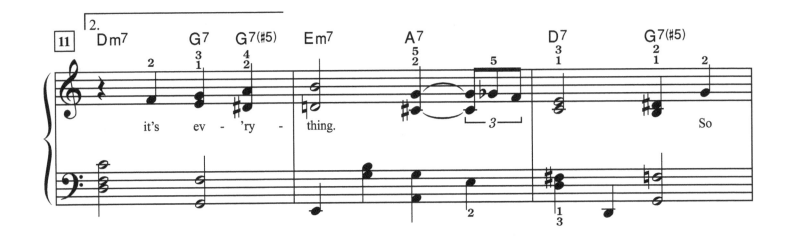

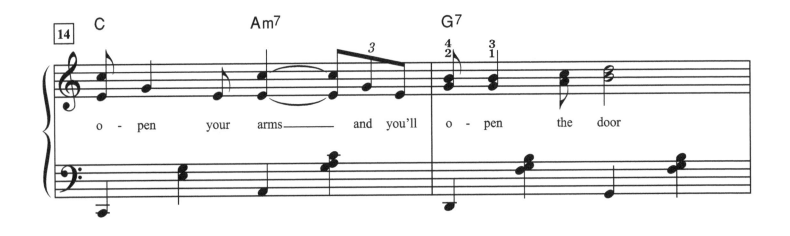

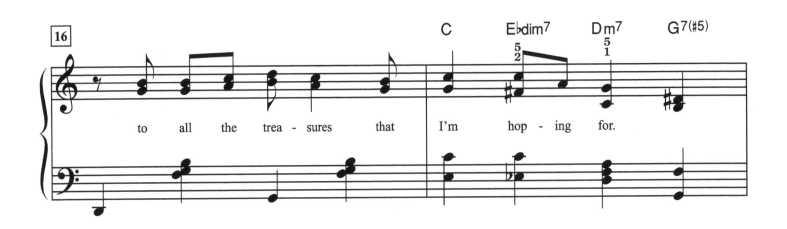

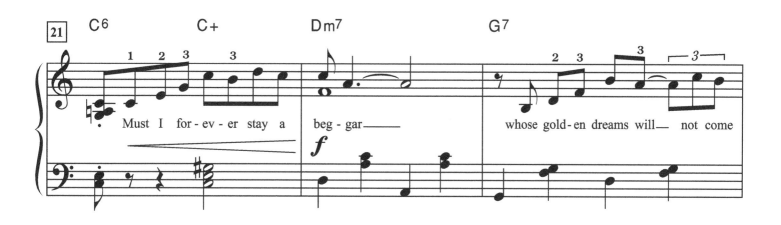

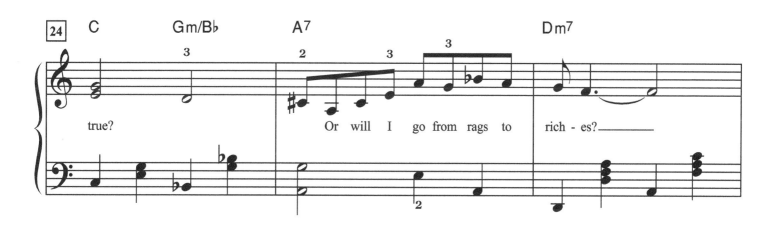

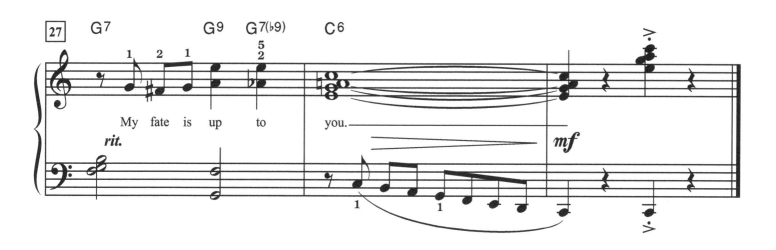

SATIN DOLL

Words and Music by
Johnny Mercer, Duke Ellington and Billy Strayhorn
Arranged by Dan Coates

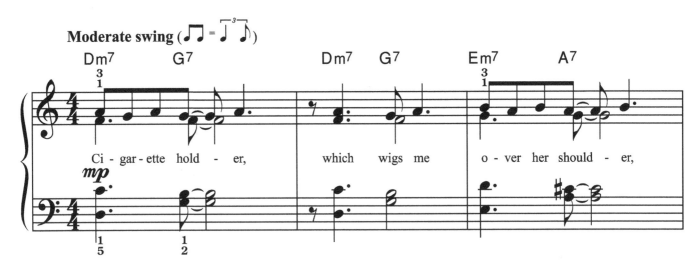

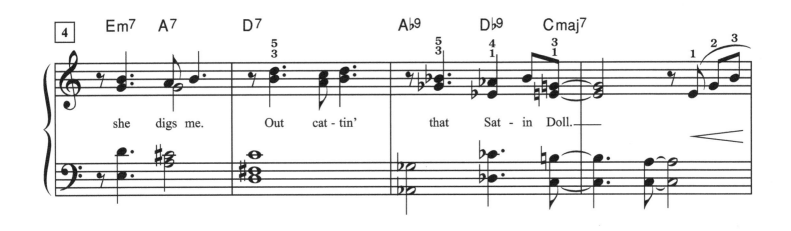

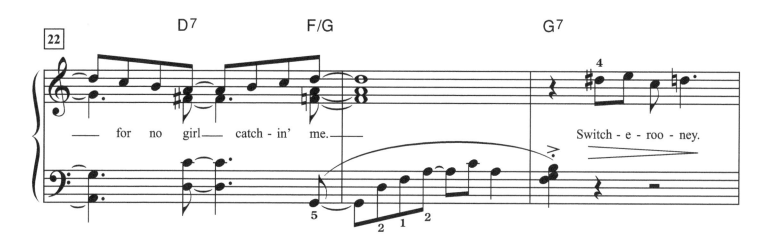

SAVE THE LAST DANCE FOR ME

Words by Doc Pomus
Music by Mort Shuman
Arranged by Dan Coates

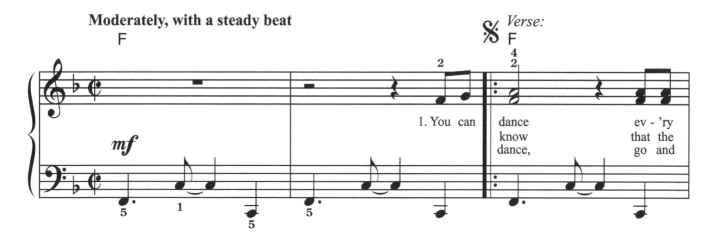

148

your hand ── 'neath the pale moon - light.──
your heart ── to an - y - one.──
take you home, you must tell him no.──

But don't for ─

Chorus:

get who's tak - ing you home and in whose arms you're gon - na be.──

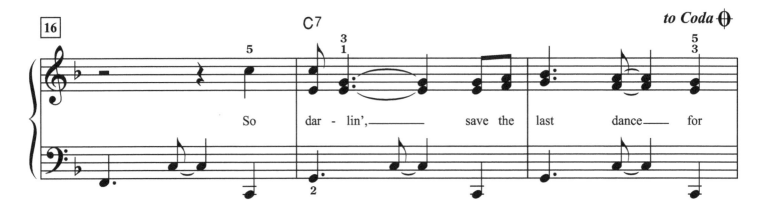

to Coda ⊕

So dar - lin',────── save the last dance──── for

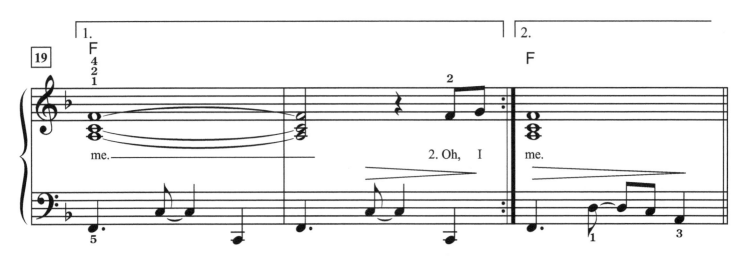

1.

me.──────

2. Oh, I

2.

me.──────

THE SHADOW OF YOUR SMILE

(from "The Sandpiper")

Lyric by Paul Francis Webster
Music by Johnny Mandel
Arranged by Dan Coates

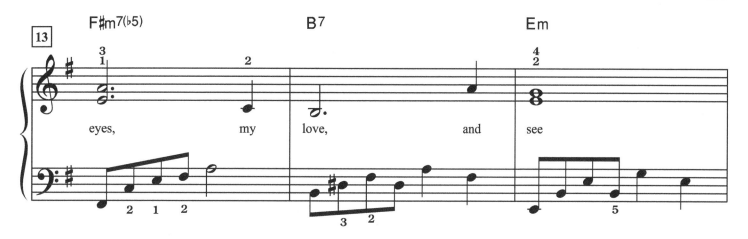

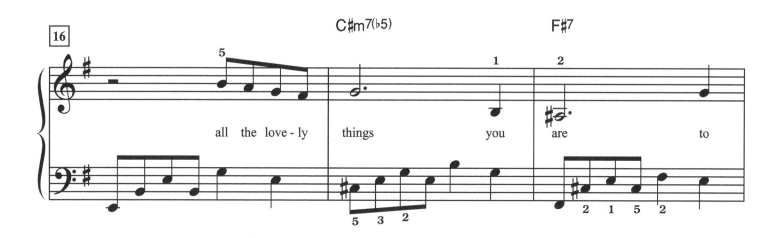

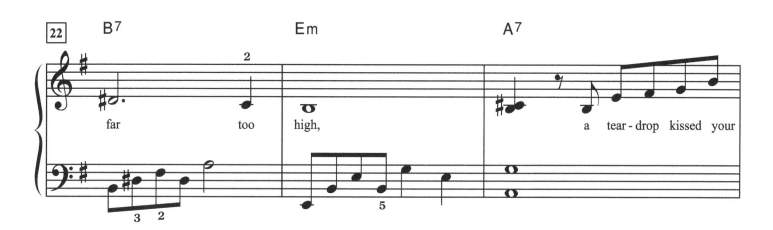

SKYLARK

Words by Johnny Mercer
Music by Hoagy Carmichael
Arranged by Dan Coates

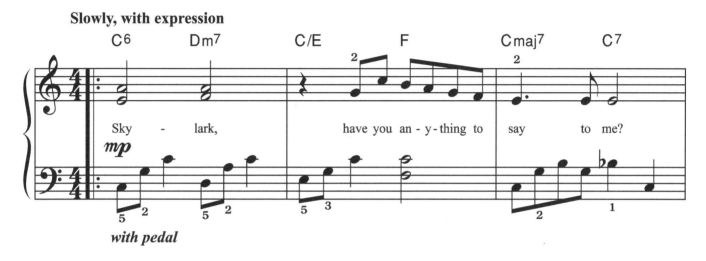

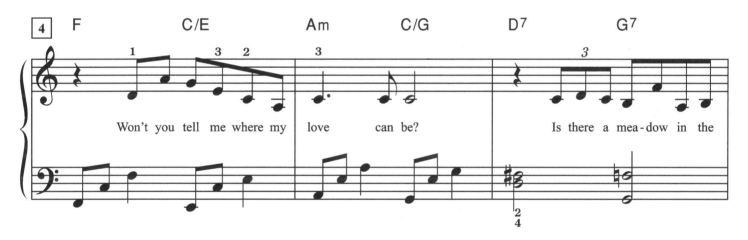

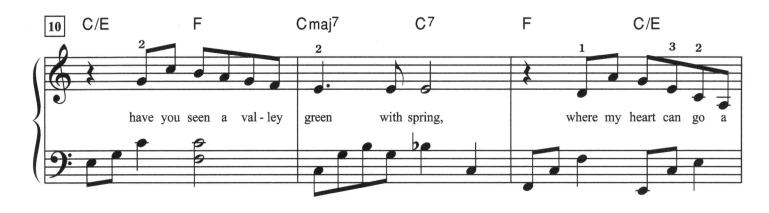

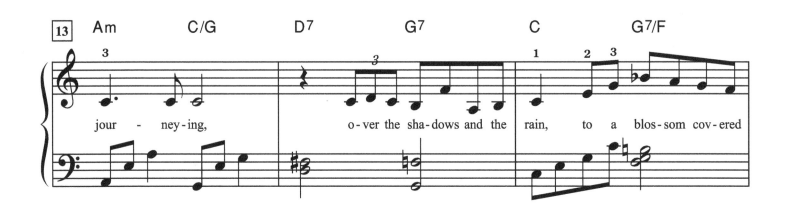

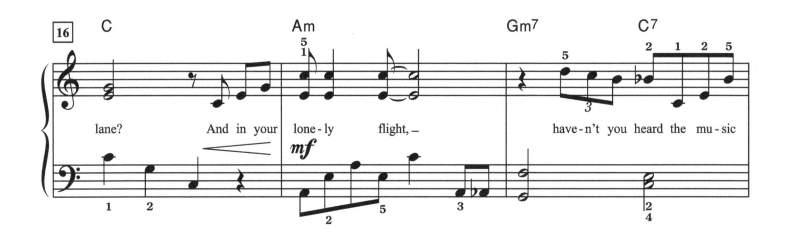

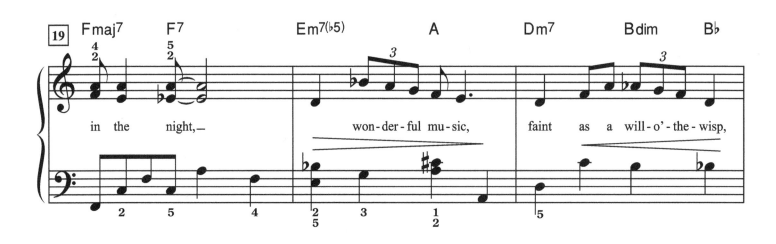

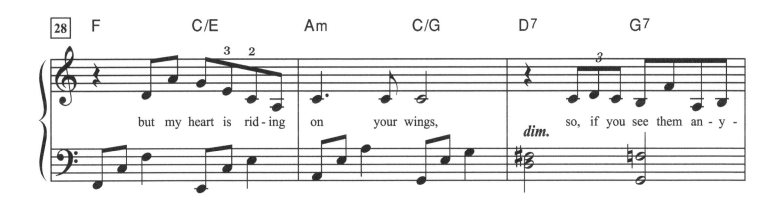

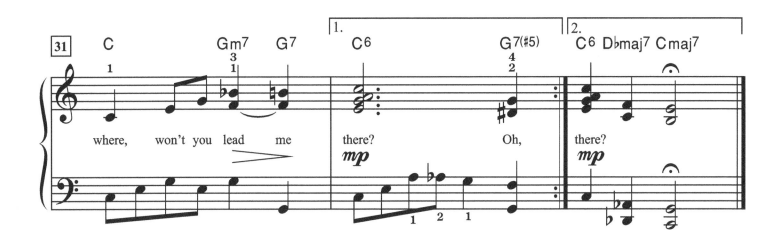

STAR DUST

Music by Hoagy Carmichael
Words by Mitchell Parish
Arranged by Dan Coates

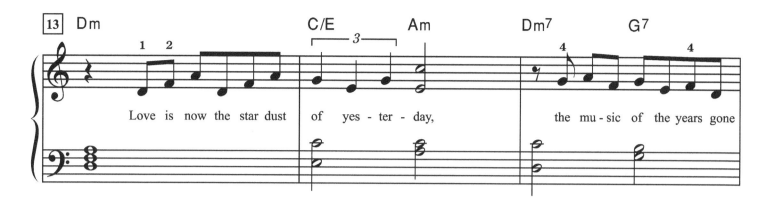

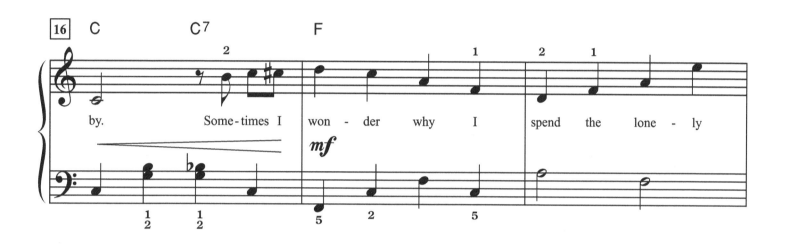

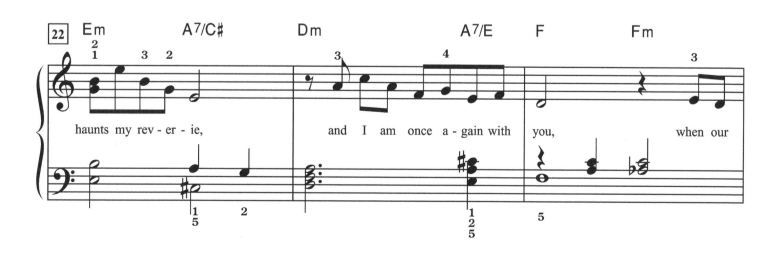

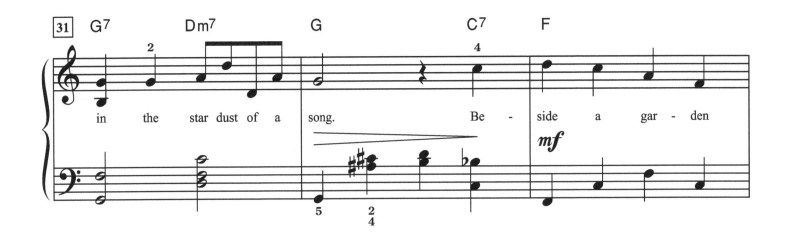

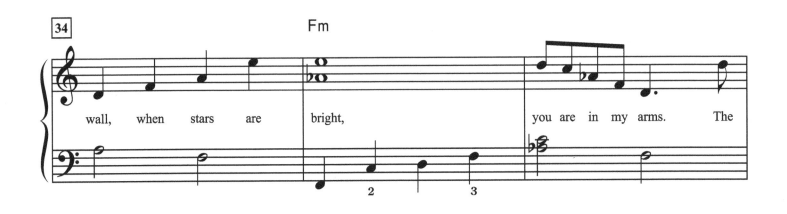

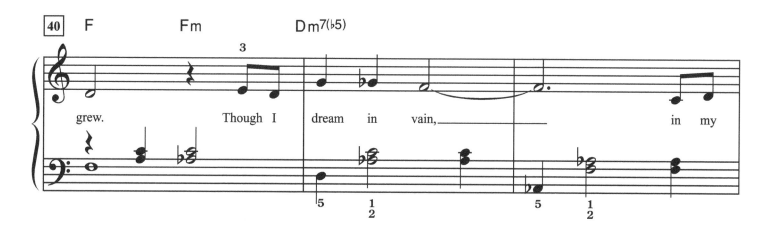

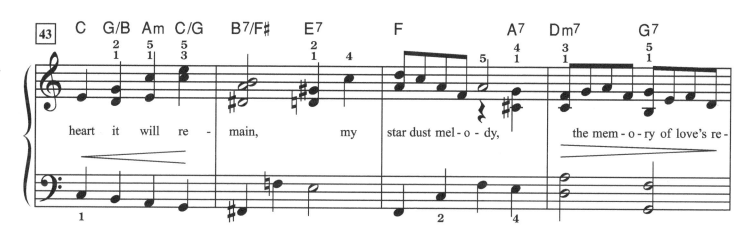

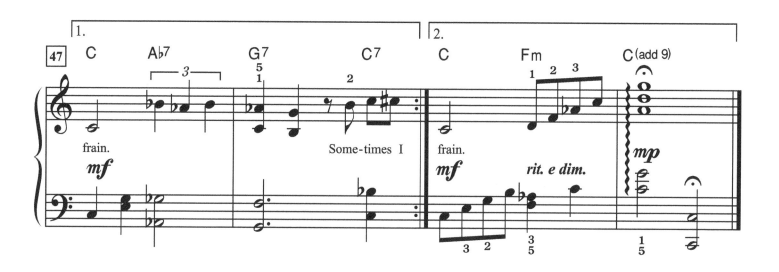

SUMMERTIME

(from "Porgy and Bess")

Music and Lyrics by
George Gershwin, Dubose and Dorothy Heyward, and Ira Gershwin
Arranged by Dan Coates

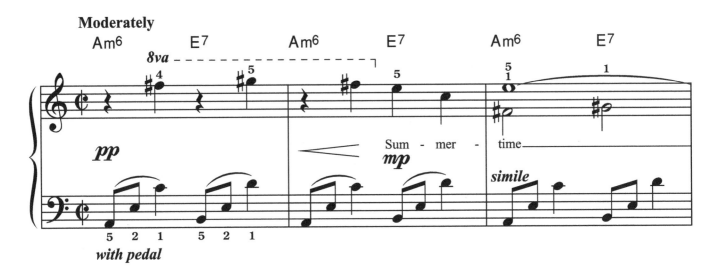

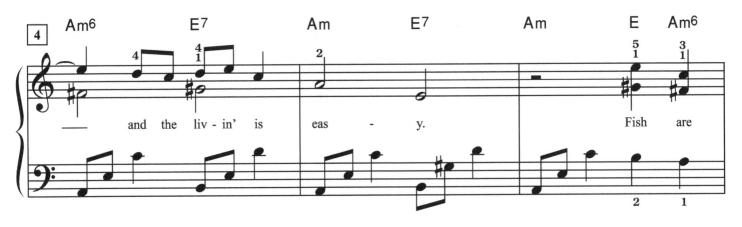

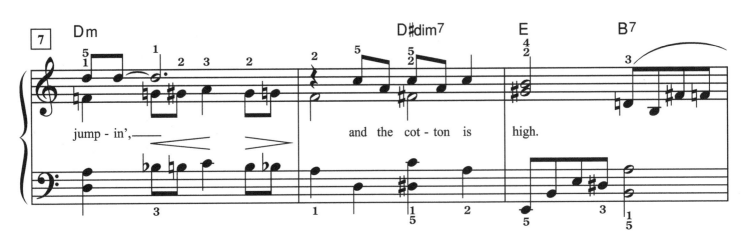

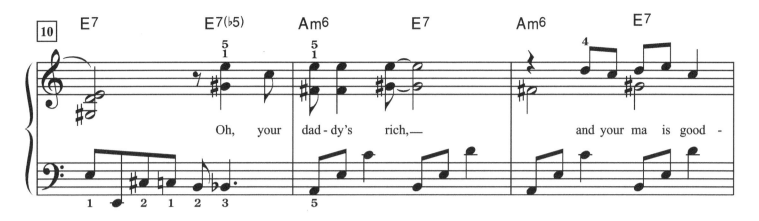

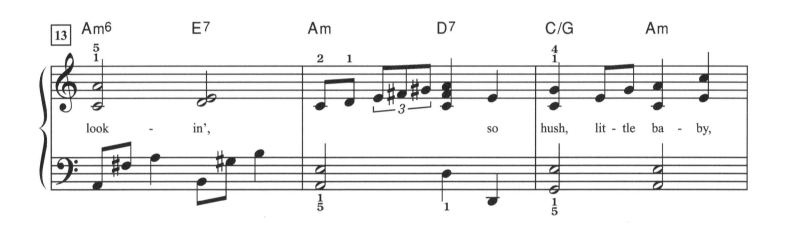

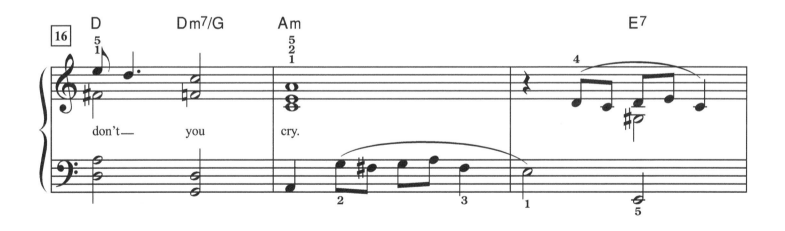

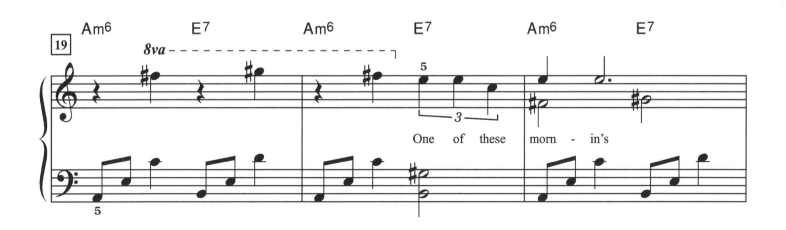

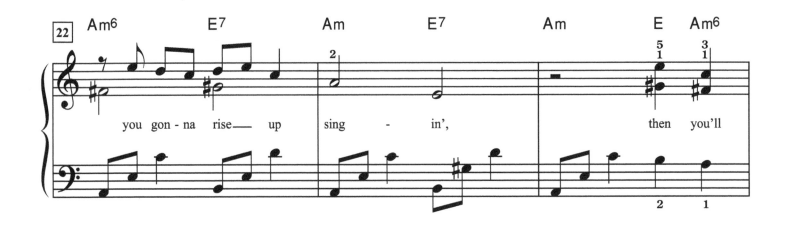

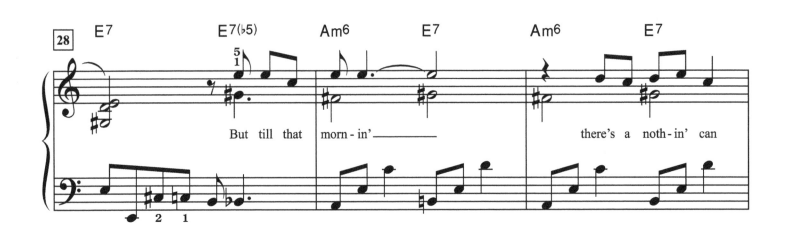

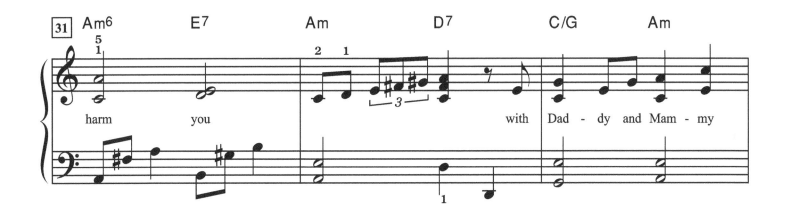

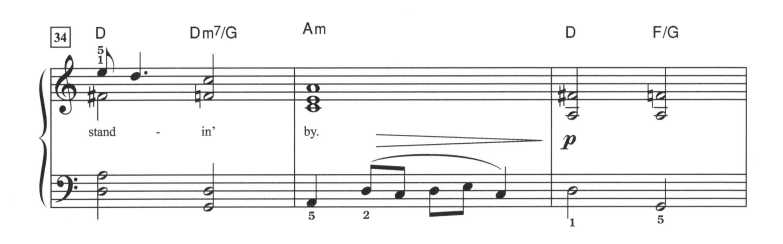

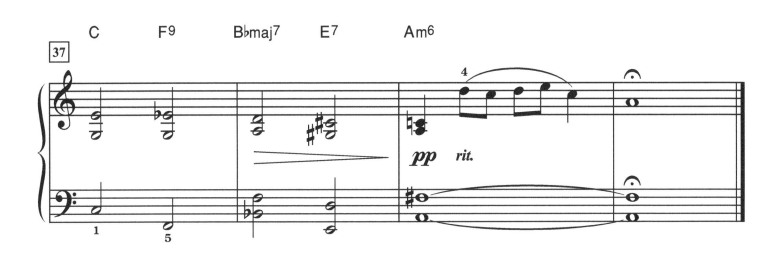

SOMEONE TO WATCH OVER ME

(from "Oh, Kay")

Music and Lyrics by
George Gershwin and Ira Gershwin
Arranged by Dan Coates

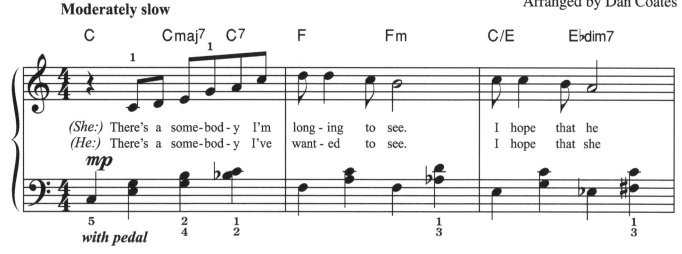

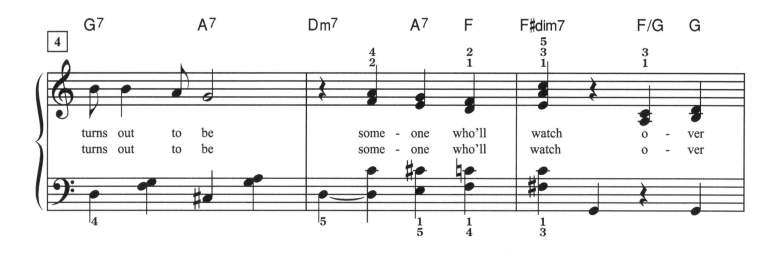

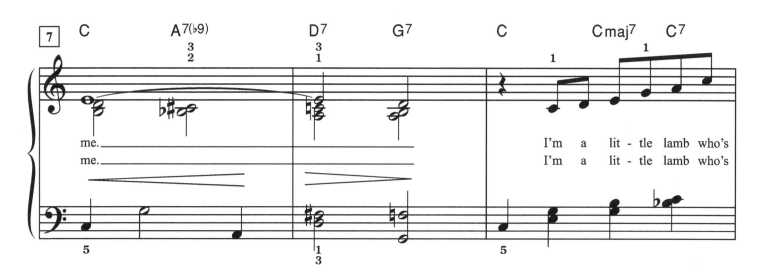

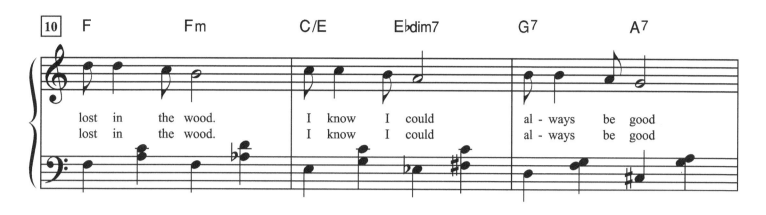

lost   in   the   wood.   I   know   I   could   al - ways   be   good
lost   in   the   wood.   I   know   I   could   al - ways   be   good

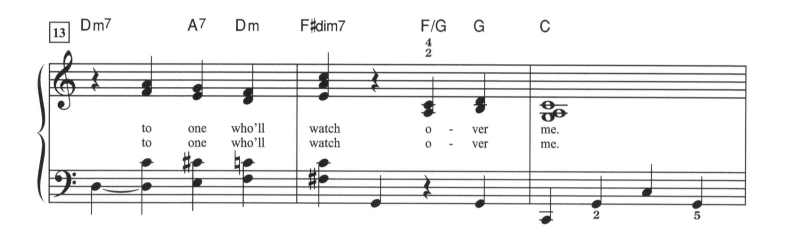

to   one   who'll   watch   o - ver   me.
to   one   who'll   watch   o - ver   me.

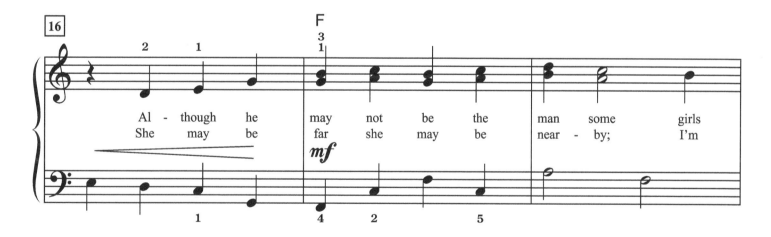

Al - though   he   may   not   be   the   man   some   girls
She   may   be   far   she   may   be   near - by;   I'm

mf

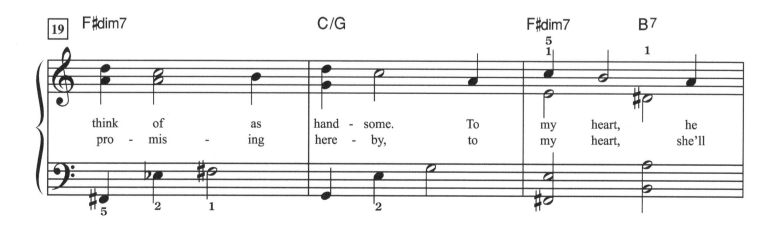

think   of   as   hand - some.   To   my   heart,   he
pro - mis - ing   here - by,   to   my   heart,   she'll

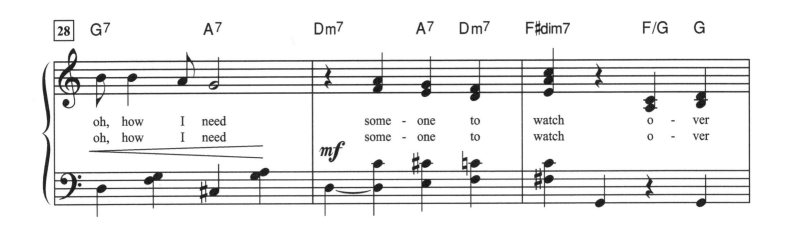

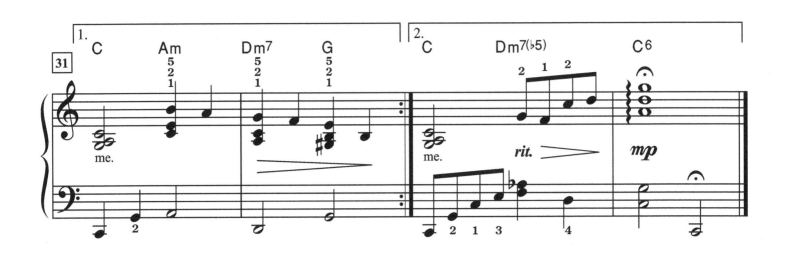

TAKE THE "A" TRAIN

Words and Music by Billy Strayhorn
Arranged by Dan Coates

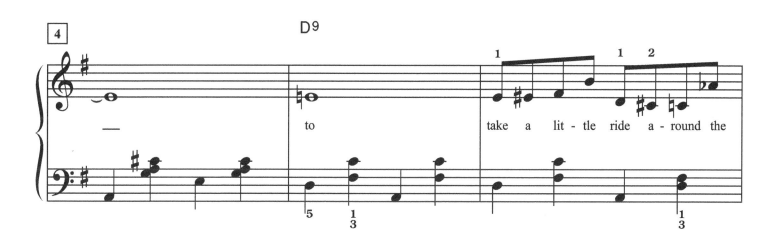

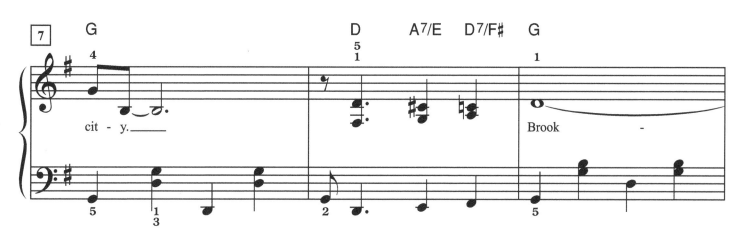

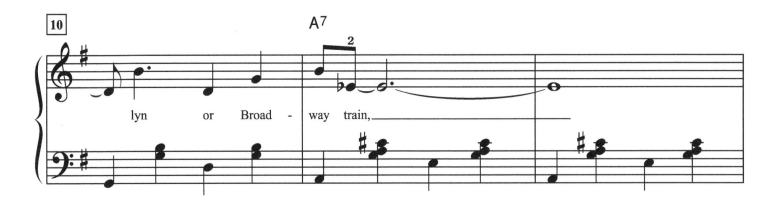

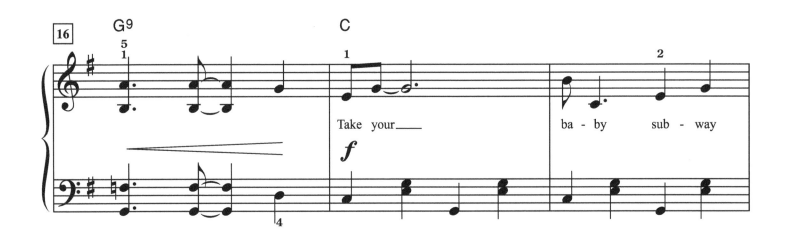

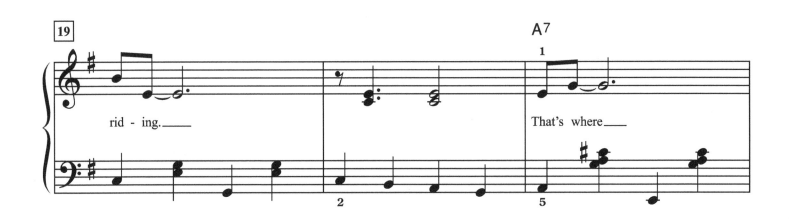

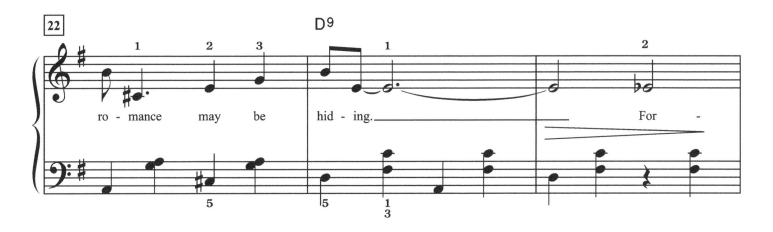

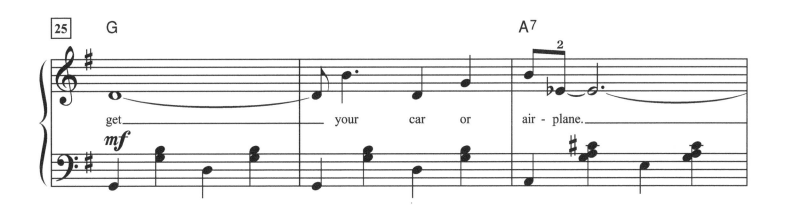

TEACH ME TONIGHT

Words by Sammy Cahn
Music by Gene DePaul
Arranged by Dan Coates

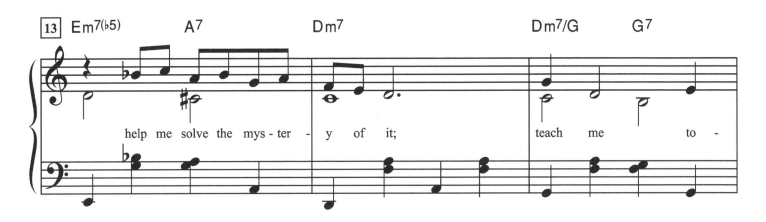

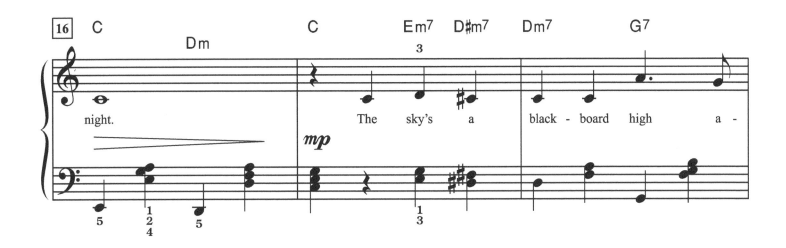

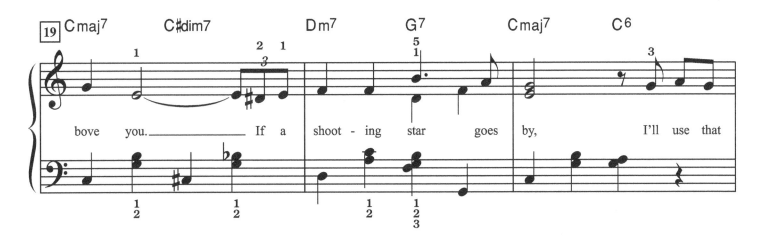

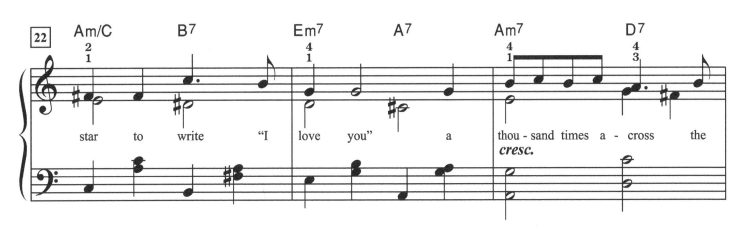

VOLARE

Music by Domenico Modugno
Arranged by Dan Coates

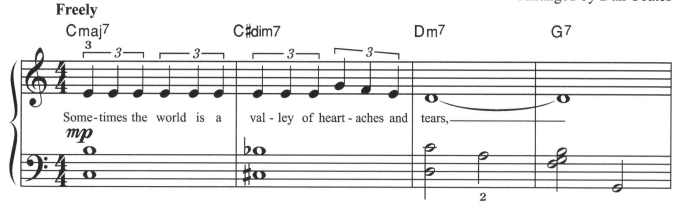

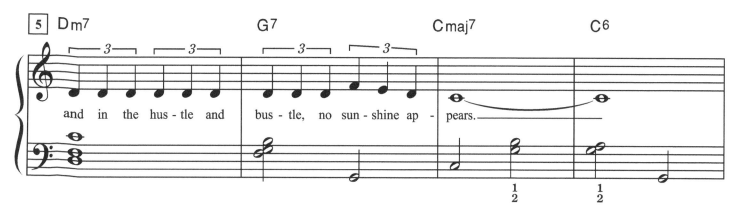

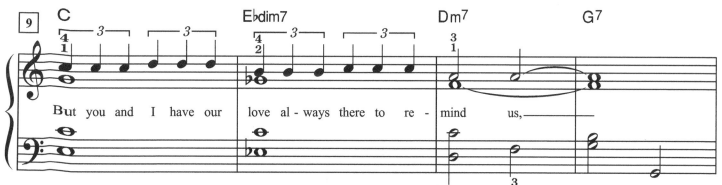

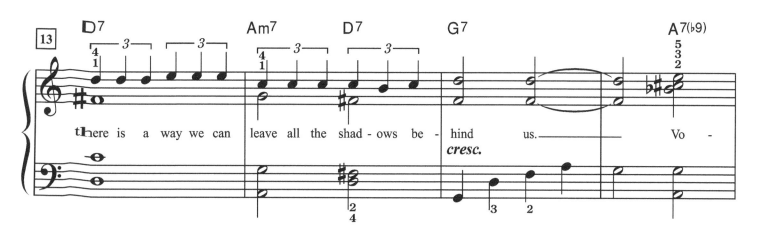